LAST CHANCE
TO SAVE OUR REPUBLIC

©Hannah Faulkner (2025)
All rights reserved.

No part of this book may be used or reproduced by any means: graphic, electronic, or mechanical, including photocopying, recording, taping or by any information storage retrieval system without the written permission of the author except in the case of brief quotations embodied in critical articles and reviews. Because of the dynamic nature of the Internet, any web addresses or links contained in this book may have changed since publication and may no longer be valid. Although every precaution has been taken to verify the accuracy of the information contained herein, the author and publisher assume no responsibility for any errors or omissions so that no liability is assumed for damages that may result from the use of information contained within. The views expressed in this work are solely those of the author and do not necessarily reflect the views of the publisher whereby the publisher hereby disclaims any responsibility for them.

Attributions
Interior Text Font: Minion Pro
Interior Title Fonts: Minion Pro
Cover Design: Aaron Farrier

Book Indexing Categories (BISAC)
SOCIAL SCIENCE: Sociology / Social Theory
HISTORY: United States / 21st Century
POLITICAL SCIENCE: Religion, Politics & State

Paperback ISBN 979-8-3304-7364-9
Hardcover ISBN 979-8-3304-7364-9
Ebook: Available on Amazon.com

Culture of 1776 Books

LAST CHANCE
To Save Our Republic

Hannah Faulkner

culture of
1776

★ ★ ★ ★ ★

Last Chance is a powerful wake-up call for all Americans to recognize and confront the deep-rooted challenges facing our Republic. Hannah highlights the critical issues, from the breakdown of the family to the erosion of moral standards, urging us to reclaim the values that once made America strong. This book is an essential read for those committed to preserving our nation's future and standing firm against the forces that seek to undermine it.

RILEY GAINES
12x All-American Swimmer
Girls Sports advocate

As a mother of 5 children, it gives me hope to see young people like Hannah stand for the truth. We live in a world that has rejected common sense, but Hannah's book '*Last Chance*' is a wake-up call for all Americans. I urge every single person that can read and is concerned about the future of America to read this book.

DR. GINA LOUDON
Author of *Mad Politics*
Host of *American Sunrise*
on *Real America's Voice*

Hannah Faulkner is a formidable force challenging the corrupt political machine intent on manipulating her generation. Her unwavering commitment to truth and her remarkable ability to reveal deception are a beacon of hope. Hannah's leadership inspires confidence that the future of our nation will be guided by principled individuals. Her book is not just a wake-up call but a powerful cry for freedom, cutting through the shadows to illuminate hope for the American dream.

DAVID HARRIS JR,
Host of *The Pulse*
on *Newsmax*

Hannah's voice is a well crying out in the middle of the desert. All who are parched must drink here.

ROSEANNE BARR
Comedy Superstar | Award-winning Actress,
Host of *The Roseanne Barr Podcast*

Last Chance is a rallying cry for "We the People" to remind us to get off the sidelines and into the fight to save our great Republic. Putting all tyrants on notice, Hannah makes the case that America is definitely worth saving. And if Hannah is an example of the next generation, America is definitely savable. This book is a firm reminder that the future is in our hands.

> DR. SIMONE GOLD, MD, JD
> Founder of AFLDS
> CEO of GoldCare

"Hannah's book, *Last Chance*' powerfully addresses the lies spread around ideas such as the 'separation of church and state', revealing the often-overlooked historical truths behind America's founding principles. This book is a compelling read for anyone seeking to understand the real intentions of the Founding Fathers and how even we got to the point where now people are confused on basic principles. I highly recommend Hannah Faulkner's eye-opening book, Last Chance!"

> WILLIAM J. FEDERER
> Nationally-known Speaker
> Best-selling Author

This book is dedicated to the men and women who have sacrificed everything for our freedom. They shed their blood, sweat, and tears—may my words honor their legacy and defend the liberties they fought to protect.

Hannah Faulkner | *October 2024*

Disclaimer

The content of this book is intended for informational and educational purposes only. While every effort has been made to ensure the accuracy and reliability of the information presented, this book represents the author's personal opinions and interpretations of American history and contemporary political events. As such, it should be understood as a work of political commentary, not as an authoritative or exhaustive historical account.

The views, analyses, and perspectives expressed herein are solely those of the author and do not necessarily reflect the views or policies of any governmental agency, institution, organization, or publisher. Readers should be aware that the subject matter discussed in this book involves complex political, social, and historical topics that may be interpreted in a variety of ways. The author encourages readers to independently verify the facts presented and assertions made and to consult additional sources before drawing conclusions or making decisions based on the information provided.

This book is not intended to provide legal, political, or professional advice, nor should any part of it be used as a substitute for consultation with qualified professionals in these fields. The publisher and the author disclaim any liability for any direct, indirect, or consequential loss or damage that may result from the use or application of the ideas, opinions, or information contained in this book. Readers are encouraged to approach the material critically and engage in open dialogue.

Additionally, while references may be made to specific events, individuals, or organizations, any resemblance to actual persons, living or dead, or actual events, beyond what is publicly known or documented, is purely coincidental. The inclusion of such references is for illustrative or critical purposes and does not imply endorsement or affiliation.

Finally, due to the dynamic and ever-evolving nature of political discourse, any web addresses, statistics, or data mentioned in this book may have changed by the time of publication. The author and publisher do not assume any responsibility for the accuracy or availability of such information after the date of publication.

Table of Contents

Disclaimer Foreword: General Flynn — i
Introduction: Last Chance — v

1 | The Founding of the American Nation — 1

2 | Silenced and Censored — 19

3 | Shall Not Be Infringed — 45

4 | The Digital Age — 59

5 | The Poison of Gender Ideology — 77

6 | Education — 105

7 | Abortion — 133

8 | The Greatest Issue Facing America — 161

9 | How Did We Get Here? — 191

Epilogue: My Message to Generation Z — 201
Acknowledgments — 210
About the Author — 213
Citations — 215
CliffNotes (Chapter-by-Chapter Research Topics) — 249
Contact — 303

Foreword
Last Chance

BY GENERAL MICHAEL FLYNN

★★★

I first met Ms. Hannah Faulkner at a Reawaken America event. She was on stage at the time as a young lady, only fifteen years of age. Hannah was speaking to an audience of five thousand, boldly and confidently, on the subjects of faith, family, and the right to life, but also touching on the moral decline in our society due to the lack of education of our youth. I was blown away at her ability to simply articulate complex issues for an audience that was on average in their fifties and sixties. She received multiple standing ovations and during her discourse with the audience you could hear a pin drop.

In this seminal book, you will learn about Faulkner and you too will be blown away by her ability to take complex societal issues and break them down in simple fashion. Faulkner's ability to teach listeners and readers transcends her young age. She is gifted beyond imagination and will be a force of leadership well into the future of our nation.

She speaks to America's founding principles and values. She describes the ideals our nation was founded on and brings to the forefront as clear an understanding of American values as I have ever understood. She describes the world we live wherein we feel almost forced into silence, submission, and censorship. She describes a pall of fear that has clouded over American society but then takes the reader back to a place of inspiration and morality. I like to call it the moral high ground; Faulkner's ability to craft a story in the digital age where we are blending the past forms of communications with the vast digital resources available to citizens globally. She especially describes—as only her youth and brilliance can do—the challenges facing us all as we attempt to navigate the minefields and trap doors we find ourselves facing in today's digital environment.

There is a "poison of ideology" that comes through in her story. This is one of the most important parts of this book. In it, she lays out the falsehoods, outright lies, and deception that impact every American—especially our youth. The latter category is being almost forced to grow up far too early instead of having the joy of growing up first as a child and then transitioning into adulthood. Every age needs to grasp what Faulkner describes in this part of her book.

On that note, education is one of the most meaningful components of her story. She describes education not as we understand it coming from our institutions, but coming from the foundation of family. The bedrock of any healthy society is clearly addressed and within it comes an honesty of what makes America such a great nation in the eyes of the rest of the world.

There are dark moments in her brilliant missive that

illustrate the evil we are up against here in America. A globalist alliance of dark, soulless forces that run the gamut of corporate, political, educational, and religious institutions that touch the lives of many of us here in America. How did we get here? What does this mean for the future? And how can we fight back against this evil?

These questions and many more are answered in this seminal story of survival and courage. As you read through these chapters, you'll learn even more about yourself. I did. My own story of persecution by a corrupt system of government that is not faceless nor nameless. The faces and names of those we are opposed to who are attempting to fundamentally transform America's constitutional republic based on Christian principles and values is under attack. We as Americans need to be fearless and Ms. Hannah Faulker brings strength, courage, commitment, and a sound understanding to every reader. You will not be disappointed as you read or listen to the rest of her story.

INTRODUCTION
Saving Our Republic

BY HANNAH FAULKNER

✯✯✯

As I began writing this book, I wanted to ensure that it wasn't solely a historical book, an opinion-based tome, or a work predominantly based on science. I wanted *Last Chance* to be a compelling combination of science, history, the Bible, and my personal experience with many of these critical issues. Above all, my prayer and hope is that this book will open your eyes to truths that the fake news media, the radical educational system, and most American churches will never tell you. As you read *Last Chance*, please don't merely scan the pages; read, digest, and highlight them. And while I have done extensive research in writing this book, I implore you to dig deeper. If we do not understand our history, we should expect to repeat it.

In the year 2024, grown men dance provocatively in front of children, people care more about feelings over facts, and society struggles to acknowledge that there are only two genders. How did we get here? Nothing changes overnight. I implore you to study the history of our decline and the significant pieces that led to where we are now. We are a laughing stock, but this Republic is still in our hands.

Throughout this book, I have highlighted some of the greatest issues facing our country today and what I believe to be the most monumental matter both now and in the future—the breakdown of the family. Before discussing any of these pressing issues, it is crucial that we understand the history of America and why "the land of the free and the home of the brave" was even founded. In *Last Chance*, I start from the birthdate of the United States when we declared our independence from England in 776. I invite you to journey with me from that beautiful, inspiring beginning to present day 2024, where corrupt politicians and immoral leaders who defend child pornography and cannot provide a simple definition of the word "woman" are the norm.

While this book is focused primarily upon America, I should add that poisonous ideologies have infected nearly all of humanity. These are global issues! However, I have specifically written about America because America is the world's leading nation. If America, the beautiful, falls, so will the others. Our founders recognized that this great nation, the United States of America, would, in fact, cease to exist if "We the People" did not put the effort into protecting this Republic. As Ben Franklin poignantly stated, "You have a Republic, if you can keep it!"

I'm a fiery young Gen Zer with a passionate message for my generation and yours. Are you a Millennial or a fellow Gen Zer? Then it's time to inculcate the moral standards found in the Holy Bible and live by them. It's time to resist liberalism and work to restore the God-given freedoms that generations of heroic men and women fought to provide us. It's time. Now.

Perhaps you're a senior member of our nation and you're grieving over the steady dismantling of the ideals that made America great. You've lived long enough to recognize that the health and fitness of America isn't improving. We're on life support, and the future is bleak. Take heart. This book is for you, too. I'm asking you to rise up, let your voice be heard, and fight once again for your children and grandchildren. Please don't quit! This nation desperately needs your voice and wisdom. Shake off the apathy and decisively act. Now more than ever, it is critically important that young and old join the fight to save America... together. But how? It's one thing to identify the problems, and it's another thing altogether to propose a plan to fix them. In nearly every chapter, I will provide an action step to give you practical ways to apply the truth presented. Join me as I revisit history, explore the present, and lay out a plan to fight for America's tomorrows. As a Christian, a conservative patriot, and a member of Gen Z, I believe wholeheartedly that we have one *Last Chance* to save our Republic. The future is in our hands.

"Our Constitution was made only for a moral and religious People. It is wholly inadequate to the government of any other."

—John Adams

*Founding Father and signer of
The Declaration of Independence*

CHAPTER 1

The FOUNDING of the AMERICAN NATION

On July 4, 1776, the thirteen American colonies declared independence from England via America's birth certificate, which is known as *The Declaration of Independence*. The fifty-six men who signed the revolutionary document were not only declaring *independence* from England; they were declaring America's *dependence* upon God Almighty. Among the many reasons for our separation from England, the chief motivation was the need for religious liberty.

This is evident when you read through many of the documents and writings from the founding era: the *Mayflower Compact*, the Charter of Rhode Island, and William Bradford's *Of Plymouth Plantation*. The Great Migration from 1620–1640 highlighted the Puritans' migration to New England in order to escape religious persecution.

By the late sixteenth century, King Philip II of Spain had brutally murdered thousands of people under the Spanish Inquisition, which was forcing Protestants to convert to Catholicism. This persecution was not unique to Spain and was experienced in England as well. In

1

fact, if you were born in proximity to the Church of England, you were a member from birth to your death bed. Around this time, the Church of England (originally established by Henry VIII) was run by the state, and—as routinely happens when governments control anything—it very quickly led to tyranny and oppression. Religious persecution was happening all across England.

By the turn of the century, under the Monarch and the ruling of King James I, it was deemed treason to break away from the Church of England. Despite this, a small group of devout Christians courageously separated themselves from the Church and began to worship God in secret. With this treasonous decision, they risked the loss of their livelihoods, their homes, and their lives.

Despite the inevitable persecution, a small underground church gathered to worship and study the Word of God at Scrooby Manor under the leadership of Reverend Richard Clyfton and Reverend John Robinson. The Separatists (known modernly as the Pilgrims) faced intense persecution and eventually knew they had to leave England in search of religious freedom.

As I write this book, I am sixteen years old, and out of the many people mentioned within the historical accounts of the Separatists, one of the most inspiring to me personally was a man by the name of William Bradford. At the age of sixteen, Bradford was forced to make a decision that would change his life forever. He could either leave the Separatist group and abandon his faith, or follow the Lord and be disowned by his family. The courageous and faithful William Bradford chose to seek and follow the Lord—a decision which led to him being disowned from his family. Bradford went on to be one of the prominent leaders of the Mayflower and a truly great influence on the religious liberty we enjoy today in America.

In late 1607, the Pilgrim Church made their first attempt to travel to Holland where religious freedom was promised. Unfortunately, the church not only failed once but twice, and many Pilgrims were caught and imprisoned because of it. On their second attempt, while embarking on the ship, many were caught by armed men. Quickly, the captain sailed away to prevent more people from being captured.

The voyage to Holland took an excruciating fourteen days amid raging wind. Providentially, one of the few remaining refugees was William Bradford, who wrote: "When man's hope and help wholly failed, the Lord's power and mercy appeared in their recovery; for the ship rose again, and gave the mariners courage again to manage her... And in the end brought them to their desired haven, where the people came flocking, admiring their deliverance; the storm having been so long, and sore in which much hurt had been done." (1)

After arriving in Holland and residing there for around a decade, they decided it was time for a portion of them to sail to America. Many Pilgrims faced economic hardships and cultural differences with others that resided in Holland. Following a series of complications, the Mayflower set sail for the New World on September 6, 1620, with 120 people on board. Rather than the trip taking the estimated three weeks, the pilgrimage took sixty-six stormy days. Throughout the voyage, the passengers trusted in the Lord for strength and provision. As they sailed to the New World, they determined that they needed a charter or a governing document, so they drafted what is known as the *Mayflower Compact*.

However, in order to create this covenant (the *Mayflower Compact*), they needed a foundation on which it was to be laid. That foundation was God Almighty. The Pilgrims recognized that the only religion that offered true freedom and liberty was Christianity. If their government were to be founded upon any other religion, it would become a monarchy, dictatorship, or theocracy. Only under Christianity does a person have the free will to choose whether or not to worship God. The Pilgrims' idea of self-government would later become the pillar of which our nation is known for: "We the People." Three profound words.

In November of 1620, the *Mayflower Compact* was signed by forty-one men aboard the Mayflower. This covenant, which was largely inspired by the Scrooby Covenant, laid the foundation for many of our founding documents, such as *The Declaration of Independence, The Constitution,* and the Articles of Confederation. Above all, the *Mayflower Compact* was the seedbed for the foundation of this country—a limited government that was represented by the people and for the people. Consider this excerpt from the *Mayflower Compact*:

> We whose names are underwritten, the loyal subjects of our dread sovereign Lord King James, by the grace

of God, of Great Britain, France, and Ireland king, defender of the faith, etc., having undertaken, for the glory of God, and advancement of the Christian faith, and honour of our king and country, a voyage to plant the first colony in the northern parts of Virginia, do by these presents, solemnly and mutually, in the presence of God and one another, covenant and combine ourselves together into a civil body politic, for our better ordering and preservation and furtherance of the ends aforesaid; and by virtue hereof to enact, constitute, and frame, such just and equal laws, ordinances, acts, constitutions, and offices, from time to time, as shall be thought most meet and convenient for the general good of the colony; unto which we promise all due submission and obedience. (2)

The hardships imposed upon the Pilgrims by the Church of England served as a schoolmaster, and by its oppression, they learned the value of freedom of thought and religion. They were persuaded that religious liberty isn't for Christians only; it is a God-given right which applies to everyone. These ideas were fundamental to the success of Plymouth Colony and the fledgling nation, but paramount to these basic freedoms was the idea and necessity of self-governance.

Self-government does not equal the abolition of civil government. In truth, you must have some sort of government or society will turn into anarchy. David Barton made a powerful statement within the pages of *The Founders' Bible,* in which he explained, "The Separatists believed that the government of Christ begins in the heart of the individual. True religious liberty could only be built upon the genuine practice of self-government... The reason is simple: self-government, by its very nature, yields peace, with 'every man under his vine and his fig tree' (1 Kings 4:25)." (3) A simple look at the history of the rise and fall of countries will reveal the necessity of limited government in order to thrive.

The Pilgrims, not unlike the Hebrews in Egypt, had learned valuable lessons from their experiences in lands of bondage. Their motherland, England, had provided them with an abundant education in governmental overreach. Almost twelve years in Holland taught them, among other lessons, the importance of protecting their children from a permissive culture.

Fast-forward about 150 years to July 4, 1776, when America officially declared its independence from England. That glorious day will be remembered forever! It marked the birth of a nation founded upon ideas inspired by God Almighty and implemented by Moses. The freedom, liberty, and prosperity encompassing these divine ideas has been described as American exceptionalism.

Alexis de Tocqueville, a French sociologist who lived in the 1800s, wrote, "The position of the Americans is therefore quite exceptional, and it may be believed that no democratic people will ever be placed in a similar one." (4) *The Declaration of Independence* reveals the six tenets of what is described as American Exceptionalism: (1) There is a Creator; (2) We have inalienable rights that come from God; (3) The government exists to protect our inalienable rights; (4) There is a fixed moral law; (5) The consent of the governed; and (6) If needed, we the people can alter, abolish, or create a new government. (5)

Barton explains, "American exceptionalism is the by-product of these six governing principles—principles that resulted in the recognition and establishment of God-given inalienable rights, individualism, limited government, religious toleration, free-market economics, full republicanism, separation of powers, checks and balances, an educated and virtuous citizenry, and other distinctive elements." (6) Ironically, Democrats push for a democracy and a large portion of Republicans push for a republic, which is what we are. Democracy almost always devolves into chaos. A republic "reps the public." We have to stop calling America a democracy.

But why is America so great? Despite the shallow opinions of Hollywood and mainstream media, millions flock to our borders. Why do they come? What do we have that they need? How did we become the freest nation in history—the land of the free and the home of the brave? Why have we been able to prosper more than any other nation over the last 250 years? How is it that we are just 4.5% of the world's population, yet we hold nearly 40% of the wealth in the entire world?

A recent statistic showed that only 16% of Gen Z is proud to be an American. (7) This statistic startles me, but it begs this question: If America is so oppressive and bad, then why are millions upon millions of people fleeing their countries to live here? Amidst all the chaos in America and issues we are facing, America is still the freest and greatest nation in the history of our planet.

I submit to you that the United States of America has been an experiment God could bless. Despite our imperfections—even at the time of our founding—this nation acknowledged the Creator and His laws from its infancy, copying God's instructions to Moses as he established the nation of Israel. Consider the words of Moses to the Israelites after their exodus from Egypt:

> Behold, I have taught you statutes and judgments, even as the Lord my God commanded me, that ye should do so in the land whither ye go to possess it. Keep therefore and do them; for this is your wisdom and your understanding in the sight of the nations, which shall hear all these statutes, and say, "Surely this great nation is a wise and understanding people. For what nation is there so great, who hath God so nigh unto them, as the Lord our God is in all things that we call upon him for? And what nation is so great, that hath statutes and judgments so righteous as all this law, which I set before you this day?" (Deuteronomy 4:5-8, KJV)

No, we aren't Israel. But an honest study of the founders' journals, letters, and books will reveal that the framework of our enduring founding documents was influenced largely by their knowledge of the Holy Bible.

> "Righteousness exalteth a nation,
> but sin is a reproach to any people."
> (Proverbs 14:34, KJV)

> "Blessed is the nation
> whose God is the Lord..."
> (Psalm 33:12, KJV)

You may ask what constitutes a righteous vs. an evil nation? First of all, it's important to clarify whose definitions of "righteous" and "evil" will be used. It is impossible to apply definitions created by men since men have shifting views and opinions. Therefore, we must yield to the unbending standard of God. He determines right from wrong, good from evil, righteous from unrighteous.

Let's dive in a little deeper. Since we understand certain actions displease God, then shouldn't we inspect the policies that represent our nation and align fully with biblical standards? If a nation can only prosper by adopting policies that honor God Almighty, then the uncomfortable yet necessary question we should ask is this: Is America honoring God with our legislation and policies? Here are a few examples.

In 1973, our Supreme Court ruled *Roe v. Wade* and the right to murder the life of your own child until "viable" legal. In 2015, our Supreme Court legalized gay marriage through *Obergefell v. Hodges*. In some states, it is legal for children to seek out genital mutilation surgery and be chemically castrated. These are just three examples. Do they comport with God's Word and submit to His commandments? No. They reveal how we, as a nation, have allowed this evil to permeate our country.

This is why it is so important that we elect biblically-literate leaders with an unyielding sense of morality and conviction. We must view our politicians as spiritual leaders. No, they are not pastors or priests, but their leadership has spiritual implications because humans are spiritual beings. None of our political leaders are perfect (nobody is), but just as King David and Solomon were spiritual leaders, so are our leaders today. I would submit to you that any man or document that governs the affairs of people is spiritual regardless of it being Christian or non-Christian. The United States Constitution is a spiritual document because it governs the affairs of men. Again, humans are spiritual beings. In contrast, the Islamic Republic of Iran has a spiritual document. It contradicts the ideas within our Constitution; nonetheless, it is still a document that is governing the affairs of men.

The United States of America has never been and never will be perfect, but it is an undisputed, historical fact that this nation was founded with God at the center of it. Barton reflects upon Tocqueville's *Democracy in America* and offers a beautiful recognition of America's virtues as he writes:

> America is not great just because of the ideas that gave her birth and the great ideals by which she lives; America has been great because for the most part she has been good. She has been the defender of freedom, a help to the needy, a rescuer of those in crisis. As opposed to a tyrannical dictator with a global hunger for conquest, she has been a benevolent force of stability and blessing to much of the world. When nations have been in big trouble, America more often than not has come to their aid as the biggest global mobilizer of help. (8)

Many often call America a democracy. America is not a democracy. We do not want a democracy. A democracy only works for a few, then once it gets to a certain size, everyone is just a peasant being led and controlled by the elites. Plato once said, "Democracy is doomed to fail because it is based on people having virtue.

But if people have to choose between giving up their life or giving up their virtue—they will give up their virtue to save their life." (9) Whereas a Republic is a "form of government in which a state is ruled by representatives of the citizen body." (10) I always get a kick out of the tweets and articles that declare that "Trump is a threat to democracy," because they are actually implying that President Donald Trump is a threat to their agenda.

America is a constitutional republic that is represented by "We the People." In January of 2023, there was considerable outrage from conservatives about Republicans not being united with Kevin McCarthy. But quite frankly, this is what our founders intended, for where there is debate, change begins. We must stop calling ourselves a democracy.

Aldous Huxley said, "The perfect dictatorship would have the appearance of a democracy, but would basically be a prison without walls in which the prisoners would not even dream of escaping. It would essentially be a system of slavery where, through consumption and entertainment, the slaves would love their servitudes. (11)

America was founded on ideas no other nation other than the commonwealth of Israel has been founded upon: life, liberty, and the pursuit of happiness. America is great because of one word—freedom. Though many refuse to give God glory for this, freedom is a biblical idea. Freedom ultimately comes from God through Jesus. No other religion in the world offers the freedom God provides.

"For you were called to freedom, brothers *and sisters;* only *do* not *turn* your freedom into an opportunity for the flesh, but serve one another through love." (12) (Galatians 5:13, NASB)

Christianity is the sole religion through which a person can experience true freedom and the idea of free will. Truly, our founders, having experienced the exploitation of England and having a reverence for the Bible, knew that the only way for people to be released from tyranny was freedom in Jesus Christ.

Although we are a nation founded on Judeo-Christian principles, we are not a theocracy. A theocracy is not biblical. We do not want a theocracy. According to Noah Webster's *American Dictionary of the English Language* published in 1828, a theocracy is a "Government of a state by the immediate direction of God; or the state thus governed." (13)

Webster explains that the Israelites furnished an "illustrious example" of a theocracy that lasted until the time of Saul. Theocracies in modern times are largely driven by fear and control, which is why we do not want a theocracy. However, in order to have a thriving nation, you must have a basis for morality, or that nation will rot from the inside out. This is exactly what our founders recognized. America has been shaped around the ideas, values, and principles found in the best-selling book of all time: the Bible. One of our late Supreme Court Justices, Justice Earl Warren, spoke at a prayer breakfast in Washington, D.C. in 1954. He uttered these words:

"I believe no one can read the history of our country without realizing that the Good Book and the spirit of the Savior have from the beginning been our guiding geniuses. Whether we look to the first Charter of Virginia, or to the Charter of New England, or to the Charter of Massachusetts Bay, or to the Fundamental Orders of Connecticut, the same objective is present: a Christian land governed by Christian principles." (14)

Additionally, our Supreme Court declared in 1931, "We are a Christian people... According to one another the equal right of religious freedom and acknowledging with reverence the duty of obedience to the will of God." (15) The overwhelming evidence from America's founding clearly shows its strong Christian roots, making it unreasonable to claim otherwise.

Sometimes I'll mention some of the previous quotes at events when I speak or when I'm debating with those in opposition, and a common argument is: "Well, those are just quotes. That doesn't mean it is actually true."

Out of approximately 15,000 documents written during our founding (1760-1805), the most quoted and cited book was the Bible at 34%, which was four times more than the second most cited book or source, which was the relative influence of European writers on late eighteenth century American political thought. (16)

Above all, the reason America was founded on Judeo-Christian values and principles is because Christianity is the only religion that offers true freedom and free will. America is great because of its unique ideas that found their origin in the Bible. If the ideas enshrined within our Constitution cease, America will no longer be great. This is why it is crucial we fight hard to protect the liberties and freedoms we have; if we lose them, America will cease to exist.

SEPARATION OF CHURCH AND STATE

More than likely, you've heard the term "separation of church and state" mentioned in the news, from college professors, and even among church folk. But interestingly, when you ask what it means or where it originated, they have no idea whatsoever. The left specifically calls "separation of church and state" like a hyperactive referee at a basketball game. Unfortunately, they blow the whistle mostly to discredit any idea rooted in Christianity. They make bad calls for the opposing team, and they typically get away with it.

One of the greatest lies and misinterpretations swallowed by secularists and church-goers alike is Thomas Jefferson's statement: "...wall of separation between Church and State." This idea is understood to mean there is a wall of separation between politics and religion. It is one of the most poisonous misconceptions people have been brainwashed into believing, and sadly, church-going Christians have believed it too. This lie has led to the removal of prayer in schools, the Bible not being read in classrooms, and the removal of God from the public square almost entirely. For the first three centuries, the two institutions (Church and State) were pretty much inseparable.

The religion of child sacrifice and the religion of hedonism are being imposed on the American people as we speak. The federal government is stealing money out of the pockets of unwitting citizens to practice child sacrifice. This is a state-run religious activity. I am not going to debate over the semantics. The State is imposing religious activity.

In Rome, the Emperor Theodosius I, also known as Theodosius the Great, reigned from 379 AD until his death and claimed he was in control, tyrannically leading both the Church and the State. He deemed Christianity the religion and made any other faith illegal. Of course, this is known as a theocracy or dictatorship, which is not biblical whatsoever. God does not force us to do what He says because He has given us free will. Emperor Theodosius and King Henry VIII of England similarly imposed a state-sponsored religion onto their people.

Reverend Thomas Hooker (1586–1647) was an important figure in early American history and was known for his leadership in the Puritan community and his contributions to the development of democratic principles in the New World. In the early 1600s, he called for a separation of the "Church and Commonwealth" because he recognized the fault in government dictating what people must believe in. Reverend Hooker played a key role in American history, specifically working to protect the church from government interference.

Fast-forward from the late 1500s to 1620, when the Pilgrims fled England to escape a state-sponsored religion being imposed upon them. They fled to America, declaring that the government had no place to impose religion or "to plant churches by power, and to force a submission to ecclesiastical government by laws and penalties." (17) They were advocates for the separation of Church and State—the kind that blocks the State's interference in Church matters.

Later, Thomas Jefferson mentioned this same idea in his "Wall of Separation Between Church and State" letter. It is critical to pay attention to the context of his letter. The idea behind this separation was to prevent the government from forcing or imposing any sort of religion onto the people. It limited the government's jurisdiction so it could not harass or place undue pressure on the Church to behave a certain way. This "wall" mentioned is a protection for the church *from* the State, which is exactly what the First Amendment of *The Constitution* does.

This separation does not mean God, Christianity, or morality should not be represented in American law. Rather, State-imposed religion should not be forced upon the people. One of the early American Methodist bishops by the name of Charles Galloway stated, "The Separation of the Church from the State did not mean the severance of the State from God, or of the nation from Christianity." (18)

Last Chance

Despite our scars and flaws, this truly is the greatest nation on earth and it is all because of its foundation upon God and His immutable laws.

*** **TAKE A** *CHANCE!* ***

If I could encourage you to read something daily, I would recommend the Founders' Bible enthusiastically. Infused with articles written by David Barton, it is an incredible combination of scripture and American history you won't find anywhere else. For those curious about our nation's founding, it provides an invaluable education that reveals insight into where our forefathers learned the principles of government enshrined in The Declaration of Independence and The Constitution.

"No amendment of the
Constitution is absolute."

—Joe Biden

CHAPTER 2

Silenced and Censored

Having read the first chapter of this book, you now understand that religious freedom was the primary motivation for the Pilgrims' immigration to America in 1620. Religious freedom is at the heart of America and has made the American Dream possible.

After touring America for nine months, Alexis de Tocqueville wrote about his observations in *Democracy in America*: "The character of the Anglo-American civilization… is the product… of two perfectly distinct elements that elsewhere have often made war with each other, but which, in America, have succeeded in incorporating somehow into one another and combining marvelously. I mean to speak of the spirit of religion and the spirit of freedom. (19) This is a powerful observation!

Religious freedom and liberty were unique in America. These freedoms couldn't be found in France, England, or really anywhere in Europe. Tocqueville went on to write: "The sects that exist in the United States are innumerable. They all differ in respect to the worship which is due to the Creator; but they all agree in respect to the duties which are due from man to man. Each sect adores the

Deity in its own peculiar manner, but all sects preach the same moral law in the name of God... Moreover, all the sects of the United States are comprised within the great unity of Christianity, and Christian morality is everywhere the same. (20)

Since the founding of America, these liberating ideas have created a nation like no other in human history. But these ideas didn't begin in 1776; they began in the hearts and minds of oppressed individuals in England who realized that God intended for people to live spiritually and physically free. Freedom truly is God's idea! When the Pilgrims fled from England due to religious persecution, they came to the New World seeking the ability to worship the Creator without fear of imprisonment, the loss of their livelihoods, or the seizure of their homes. In England, they were muzzled and forced to meet secretly with no ability to speak freely.

Consider the charter of Roger Williams' Colony of Rhode Island, which happened to be one of the first documents written in America in the year 1663: "No person within the said colony, at any time hereafter, shall be in any way molested, punished, disquieted or called in question, for any differences in opinion in matters of religion, and who do not actually disturb the civil peace of our said colony; but that all... may from time to time, and at all times hereafter, freely and fully have and enjoy his and their own judgements and consciences, in matters of religious concernments. (21)

This was over one hundred years before America had officially declared independence from England in 1776, but this document was laying the foundation for the freedom to speak without restriction as enumerated in the First Amendment.

Best-selling author and radio host, Eric Metaxas, wrote, "The government essentially said, 'Yes, be religious. We will not only tolerate it; we will respect it, and we will encourage it. But we cannot take sides or put our thumbs on the scales.' But the understanding of this has been lost to many in modern America. (22)

The Pilgrims left Europe to escape an establishment of religion and the suffocating persecution that accompanied it. If you did not subscribe to the state religion, things would turn upside down for you. Any opponents who didn't march in lockstep with the Anglican Church were either fined, harassed, or put in jail. Conversely, the United States Constitution simply says that the government cannot "establish" or impose any religion onto the people.

The First Amendment to the United States Constitution reads, "Congress shall make no law respecting an establishment of religion, or prohibiting the free exercise thereof... (23)

If our freedom to express our religious beliefs is lost in America, every single other right we have will also be lost. Having the freedom to speak and practice our own religion is crucial in order to have a successful nation. If you cannot speak freely, what does freedom even mean? What constitutes the idea of freedom if you aren't allowed to worship and practice your religion of choice? Unfortunately, today, the concept of speaking freely has been forgotten by many of our politicians and elected representatives. Not only is the United States government imposing religion onto its people, it is actively stripping citizens of their constitutional right to speak and express their religious beliefs without hindrance. Let me be clear. A society cannot thrive without a firm foundation dependent upon God.

The 2020 PLANdemic

In 2020, during what many now call the "PLANdemic," the elites shut down our churches, labeling them non-essential, and punished, fined, and stigmatized devout Christians as criminals for publically worshiping God. All the while, they allowed bars, strip clubs, casinos, liquor stores, and the like to remain open. Remarkably, the progressive agenda seeks to remove our dependence upon God and replace it with a dependence upon the government.

In May of 2020, the city of Chicago started fining churches that did not "comply" with the Governor's statewide stay-at-home order. (24) In the state of Illinois, religious services and churches as a whole were deemed "non-essential" and were limited to less than ten attendees. On April 12, 2020, the Governor of Illinois, JB Pritzker, posted on X (formerly known as Twitter): "April hosts many important celebrations for some of the largest religions. I know how hard it is to break from traditional celebrations of togetherness. But I believe passionately that adapting our expressions of faith in these times is one of the most faithful acts of all. (25) Notice how this governor is using a fallacious emotional appeal to portray Christians as unfaithful bad guys for wanting to gather and express the religious freedom afforded to us by *The Constitution*.

Matt Staver, the founder and chairman of Liberty Counsel, cleverly responded to Gov. Pritzker in an interview with *Fox News*, "Governor Pritzker clearly does not seem to know that churches have the First Amendment right to exist. (26)

Throughout that unprecedented assault on religious freedom during the 2020 COVID shutdowns, it was disturbing to witness churches and pastors use the phrase "love your neighbor" in reference to wearing a mask. In a blog published by a Christian organization, *Raising Everyday Disciples,* the author wrote about whether or not she wanted to wear a mask:

> As these thoughts and emotions rolled through my mind, I had to continually preach the truth of Mark 12:31 to myself: "Love your neighbor as yourself… love your neighbor as yourself…" Over and over as

I grabbed my groceries, I had to continue to tell this truth to myself because I know that wearing a face mask is one very practical way that I can be loving my neighbor above myself in this crazy season of a pandemic across the globe. Often, loving our neighbor above yourself takes sacrifice and discomfort (And really, compared to many across the globe, this is a tiny, little sacrifice of discomfort I'm having to make!). As I walked the isles, I was drawn to think of how Jesus loved us above Himself and sacrificed His own comforts for our sake. (27)

This was a consistent, warped message from many evangelical leaders throughout the pandemic.

According to God's Word, I am to love my neighbor as myself. The Bible does not teach us to jeopardize our health in order to love others, thereby putting ourselves in spiritual or physical danger. It is my core belief as a Christian that wearing a mask is not only physically unhealthy, it is spiritually unhealthy. I believe that masks are oppressive and dark. Masks restrict relational intimacy and interpersonal communication. Expressions are limited, and smiles are not exchanged. They are dangerous for people with pre-existing respiratory issues, making it difficult for them to breathe. Most especially, forced masking is communistic and infringes upon self-governing individuals' rights to the freedom to choose what they do or do not deem necessary for their own well-being. Those were my beliefs back when they were considered "conspiracy theories." Now it's simply a widespread truth. Masks are ineffective. Period.

It is also my belief that no one should have to obtain a religious exemption if they do not want to inject a vaccine into his or her body. If I do not want a drug or vaccine, I don't want a drug or vaccine. It is that simple. No one should force any individual to inject a drug into their body, and no one should have to provide their employer with a religious exemption. This is not Communist North Korea, this is the United States of America! We are free humans with free wills! Our unalienable rights include life, liberty, and the pursuit of happiness! Forcing Americans to mindlessly inject a vaccine or any other drug that they do not deem necessary or advantageous to their health infringes upon their right to life, and stripping Americans of their right to self-govern infringes upon their right to liberty. The United States government does not own me, nor do they own you. The corporations do not own me, nor do they own you.

The fact that people lost their livelihoods, their licenses to practice medicine, and their careers as honorable military personnel over refusing a rushed and unproven vaccine is proof that we are in danger. We have allowed Marxist, communist, and socialist ideas to take over our country.

The pandemic was, among other things, a spiritual attack. God does not want us six feet apart with our fac-

Silenced and Censored

es muzzled, staying quarantined in our homes. We were created for fellowship and community, and—as Christians—we have been commanded by God to assemble in corporate worship. Everything that happened during the pandemic was in direct opposition to that. I can assure you that Satan—our enemy—wants us isolated, quarantined, and separated from others. He wants us to be confused and misdirected while God offers us His timeless wisdom.

THE MUZZLING OF RELIGIOUS FREEDOM

One of the most popular Supreme Court cases surrounding religious freedom was *Masterpiece Cakeshop Ltd v. Colorado Civil Rights Commission*. The baker, Jack Phillips, allegedly violated the Colorado Anti-Discrimination Act (CADA) shortly after two gay men (Craig and Mullins) filed a complaint against the baker for refusing to bake a cake for their "wedding." An administrative law judge in Colorado heard the case. Phillips made it clear that requiring him to bake this cake would clearly violate his First Amendment right to free speech and his right to express his religion without being silenced or punished by the government. Essentially, he believed the government had no business "compelling him to exercise his artistic talents to express a message with which he disagreed. (28) Not only did the baker win this case, religious liberty and freedom won! Phillips was allowed to exercise his

First Amendment right to decide which customers his bakery would accept.

The American Bar Association came out with a statement regarding this case stating:

> All antidiscrimination statutes pose a tension between equality and liberty. Any law that prohibits discrimination—whether based on race or sex or religion or sexual orientation or any other grounds—denies the freedom to choose who to serve or to hire. Indeed, this was a key objection to the Civil Rights Act of 1964, which prohibits places of public accommodation from discriminating based on race and forbids employers from discriminating based on race, sex, or religion: The law interferes with the freedom to choose one's customers or employees. Congress and the courts both deemed ending discrimination to be more important than protecting the right to discriminate. (29)

Another similar but more recent case highlighting our jeopardized freedom of religion in America was *303 Creative LLC v. Elenis*. Lorie Smith was the owner of a design studio, 303 Creative, where she specialized in website and graphic design. Ms. Smith started her own small business shortly after she left the corporate world with the hopeful goal of being able to embrace and promote her values through her business. She had the vision to expand her portfolio and begin designing websites for traditional married couples, and this mission fully aligned with her values. However, Colorado, as seen in the previous story with the baker, has shown that they are unconcerned with protecting the First Amendment of our United States Constitution. Essentially, the State of Colorado was attempting to force Smith to portray beliefs (same-sex marriage) through her art that were contrary to her own values. Fortunately, freedom of speech and religion won again in this case when the Supreme Court, in a six-to-three decision, reversed the lower courts, recognizing that Lorie Smith or any business owner in general has the First Amendment right to choose who they will or will not work for.

The Supreme Court said, "The First Amendment's protections belong to all, not just to speakers whose motives the government finds worthy... The First Amendment prohibits [the government] from forcing a website designer to create expressive designs speaking messages with which the designer disagrees. (30) The court added, "Consistent with the First Amendment, the Nation's answer is tolerance, not coercion. The First Amendment envisions the United States as a rich and complex place where all persons are free to think and speak as they wish, not as the government demands. (31)

Ms. Smith's victory truly was a win for all Americans' religious liberty and freedom. However, it is disturbing that we are debating whether or not people can practice their faith in and outside of their privately-owned businesses and that three Supreme Court justices (Sotomayor, Kagan, and Brown Jackson) voted against freedom of speech and the majority court's opinion. Justice Gorsuch responded to them: "Perhaps the dissents find these possibilities untroubling because it trusts state governments to coerce on 'enlightened' speech. But if that is the calculation, it is a dangerous one indeed." The bottom line is, "The dissent abandons what th[e] Court's cases have recognized time and time again: A commitment to speech for only *some* messages and *some* persons is no commitment at all. (32)

Penny Nance, the CEO of Concerned Women for America responded to the threat against religious freedom in a CBN News interview: "Religious freedom is a universal human right that was endowed by our Creator. A state cannot give it, and a state cannot take it away. It comes from God. (33)

Another attack on our religious liberty and freedom of speech is ESG, which stands for Environmental, Social, and Governance. Essentially, ESG is a set of standards which measures the "wokeness" of a company. The higher the score, the greater the access to capital, credit, and other financial perks. The million dollar question is: How can a company achieve a higher ESG score? You guessed it. By adopting policies like affirmative action, which hires and fires people based on their gender and the color of their skin. It's inherently discriminatory and racist. Other policy examples are abortion travel expenses. If a woman resides in a state with strict abortion laws, abortion travel expenses provided by her employer enable her to travel across state lines to murder her unborn child. I could supply many other examples of how ESG is pressuring corporations and companies, tantalizing them with the irresistible American dollar. Companies are changing their internal policies daily to meet these leftist ideologies. To put it simply, ESG is corporate socialism. DEI (Diversity, Equity, and Inclusion) is corporate socialism. If you have a business that doesn't align with ESG—but the bank you need a loan from fully embraces ESG—your business is most likely going to be considered a "bad investment."

Imagine an economy that is ESG-controlled. American business ideas would be weak and "woke." The dreadful consequence for consumers is a nation that devalues and dehumanizes the unborn and harms hard-working Americans who don't align with this radical, leftist ideology. This is not freedom! ESG is an attack on religious liberty as it awards and punishes those with specific beliefs.

But what can we do about ESG and its impact upon Americans?

First of all: put pressure on these businesses and corporations whenever you have the chance through boycotting. Remember how the country banded together to boycott Bud Light when they put a man who thinks he is a woman (Dylan Mulvaney) on a beer can? Secondly,

I recommend supporting small businesses and farmers. Put your money and resources into family-run businesses who align with your values. It may cost a bit more, but nourishing ESG-controlled corporations will cost the American people our precious freedoms.

The United States government is imposing state-sponsored religions onto "We The People." Abortion is an infringement of our religious freedom. The federal government funds Planned Parenthood, which provides teens with abortions, birth control, contraceptives, and more without informing parents or receiving their consent. The government is weaponizing the public school system to pump controversial, anti-family ideologies like gender theory and critical race theory into the next generation's hearts and souls.

Many of you may be familiar with the boy nicknamed the "backpack kid," who had the Gadsden flag on his backpack. (34) In August of 2023, a young twelve-year-old student by the name of Jaiden was removed from his class for the "offensive" patch on his backpack. The Gadsden flag patch was deemed "disruptive" due to its "origins with slavery." The school ordered the twelve-year-old to remove the patch, but the boy stood unwaveringly firm on his beliefs. Within just a few days of his suspension from class, the school apologized.

A Catholic pro-life volunteer by the name of Isabel Vaughan-Spruce was arrested in Birmingham, England, for silently praying outside a closed abortion clinic. Prior to the arrest, an officer informed her that silently praying is an "offense" against the Public Spaces Protection Order that bans protest by "graphic, verbal, or written means, prayer or counseling. (35) While this story didn't occur in America, I am sharing it because this same thing is happening in the United States of America.

The Biden Regime's Department of Justice convicted and imprisoned an elderly woman (age 74) for protecting the unborn. Joan Bell, alongside others, was found guilty of violating the FACE Act (Freedom of Access to Clinic Entrances Act). This act essentially prohibits any individual from interfering with someone "obtaining or providing reproductive health. (36) According to an article by Focus on the Family, Joan Bell was married to Chris Bell, who is the founder of Good Counsel, an organization which provides love, support, housing, etc., to pregnant women in need. The couple had helped nearly 8,000 women who had found themselves in crisis. Lila Rose tweeted: "At the age of 74, Joan is facing up to a decade in prison for protesting the slaughter of babies old enough to survive outside of the womb and a man who admitted on camera his willingness to commit infanticide... In the face of this injustice Joan has simply stated: 'I'm humbled by the privilege to suffer... imprisonment for the little babies.'" (37) In twenty-first century America, a 74-year-old wife and mother is being imprisoned for protecting the innocent's right to life, liberty, and the pursuit of happiness while those who destroy pregnancy clinics, Catholic churches, and pro-life centers are rarely punished for their actions. This is the result of a weaponized DOJ.

Mr. William Thomas, who now identifies as Lia, is a male swimmer who was allowed to compete on a women's team. Allowing him to compete on the women's team brought disturbing ramifications to our freedom of speech. The universities used fear tactics to silence the women on the teams, threatening that if they dared to speak out they would "regret it." Many were told they could possibly lose scholarships or future career opportunities if they vocalized concerns about Thomas swimming. Paula Scanlan, a swimmer at the University of Pennsylvania, conducted an interview with a staffer at the Independent Women's Forum and stated:

> It wasn't until the media really started picking up that the athletic department came in and actually sat us down and had a team meeting and told us to stay away from the media. Which I thought was very interesting, because I think they should've definitely addressed it earlier if that's what they wanted us to do, but it was already many months into the season that they decided to actually formally have a chat with us about what was going on, and how, "There's nothing we can do to get Lia off the team. Lia will be completing the season no matter what. You guys just have to be okay with that. (38)

The interviewer asked when the news and general public started to become aware of this, and Paula replied:

It really started blowing up in the media at the beginning of December. We got an email from an assistant to the athletic director saying, "Hi, girls," addressed only to the women's team. "Team meeting in the stands, 4:00, everyone mandatory. You need to be there." And the interesting part about this is every other team meeting we've ever had has been set up by the captains or the coaches, so the fact that the athletic department was the one who sent this email... and I have the email proof that they did book this meeting... was very weird. And so I was in the early slot of practice, so that meant I practiced before the meeting happened, and I was so anxious because I had no idea what they were going to say, but I knew it wasn't going to be good. So, we go to this meeting, and there was, like, 10 people standing there. There was our coaches, there was multiple people from the athletic department, there was someone from the LGBT center, someone from the psychological services, and... Yeah, I think that was pretty much the panel of people that were there. And they just said a few things. The main takeaway was, "Don't talk to the media. They're not your friend. You will regret speaking to the media." Another thing they said is, "Lia swimming is non negotiable." And the third thing they said is, "If you have issues with that, here are the resources that can help you be okay with that," one of which, they offered us psychological services. So, I thought that it was very interesting that they were suggesting that we needed therapy in order to be okay with the situation, and that was definitely the most concerning. I mean, the rest of the people that were there like, okay, I would've expected them to say not to talk to the media. Every other team in the Ivy League, and other teams, were told the same thing. Riley was told the same thing at the University of Kentucky. But, I think the fact that they brought in psychological services was so, so, so scary, because it was basically suggesting that we needed to be re-educated. That's the way I took it. It was... They were suggesting they needed to have re-education. And again, like you mentioned, a lot of communist countries were doing that. And again, I didn't take them up on that. I don't think anyone did, but I would've been very curious to know what they would've said in a therapy session, had you gone and talked to them about this. (39)

This is the epitome of bullying. Fear tactics designed to keep these innocent young ladies from expressing their beliefs or opinions on the matter, combined with the suggestion that they might need psychological services is outrageous. These outlandish stories seem like fake news or Babylon Bee sarcasm, but they aren't! This craziness is actually happening. Academia and the United States government are silencing young female athletes for speaking out against men—not just competing against them in their sports but undressing in their locker rooms. It is almost as if we are truly living in George Orwell's *1984*, where critical thinking is a crime. If you ask questions, you are silenced. If you take action, you are punished. (I will dive more deeply into gender ideology in Chapter 5.)

President Obama

If I were to quantify each former president's anti-religious liberty actions and compare them, President Barack Obama would top the charts as the supreme offender. The policies his administration implemented "represent the greatest government-directed assault on religious freedom in American history." (40)

The Union of Orthodox Jewish Congregations of America replied, "Most troubling is the Administration's underlying rationale for its decision, which appears to be a view that if a religious entity is not insular, but engaged with broader society, it loses its 'religious' character and liberties... The Administration's ruling makes the price of such an outward approach the violation of an organization's religious principles. (41)

What happened on January 6, 2021, is really the perfect example of how freedom of speech is being stripped away completely. That day, nearly one million Americans were peacefully protesting what many now believe to be the stolen election of November, 2020. In return, they were punished for expressing their constitutional right to speak freely. This peaceful protest began to get violent when Capitol police began inciting violence to the unarmed Americans, killing Ashli Babbitt, Kevin Greeson, Benjamin Phillips, and Rosanne Boyland. Over 900 innocent protestors have been politically persecuted by the corrupt Biden administration as well as the FBI. Some have spent over twenty months in 23-hour solitary confinement.

January 6 was not an insurrection. No one brought weapons, and no one in attendance killed a single person. But the question I have asked and continue to pose is this: If January 6 was all the Republicans' fault, and if it was an insurrection, then why would they want to hide footage from us? The answer to this simple question tells us all we need to know. January 6 was not an insurrection; it was an inside job. All you have to do is look at the video footage. Capitol police allowed people in and escorted them through the halls. The government is consistently lying to the American people and making it out to be the MAGA patriots' fault. Antifa, the FBI, and uniparty had their hands in this to trap conservatives. The global elites have one goal in mind: to control through a one-world government. They have successfully silenced us and made us out to be the "bad guys" through Big Tech, the media, and Hollywood, which will be dissected in greater detail later.

The bottom line is that Democrats (and even a large part of the Republicans) do not care about the truth. Every single person with half a brain knows that January 6 was set up by the Democratic Party so that they could have a talking point to make patriots look like the crazy ones. The National Guard was turned down by Nancy Pelosi. Capitol police walked people in and throughout the Capitol Building. Qanon Shaman, one of the protestors there on January 6, walked in and out peacefully. He was wrongfully put in prison.

During the BLM George Floyd riots throughout 2020, nearly seventy people were murdered and small businesses and towns were destroyed. Damages exceeded two billion dollars, and all the communist Democrats wanted to talk about was January 6. Does anyone care about justice and truth?

The 2020 Election

Looking back at the 2020 election as a whole, it is abundantly clear that the left used Big Tech and the media to censor conservatives while increasing the push of their agenda. In 2022, an FBI agent testified to several Republican attorney generals that the FBI was holding weekly meetings with multiple Big Tech companies in Silicon Valley. This was held near and before the 2020 presidential election to discuss the "disinformation" that was being spread by "right-wing" conservatives. They discussed the actions that needed to be taken in order to censor that information. (42)

Every single person involved in this should be in prison for at least three to five years. It would put a stop to this immediately. This is what you call white collar crime.

In a discussion with *Fox News,* Attorney General Jeff Landry stated, "Americans should be angered that during the 2020 election cycle, federal agencies peddled information that has since been disproven... No American should be censored by the government." (43)

I have witnessed unpleasant political and religious persecution in my immediate family. In the spring of 2022, my brother was playing on a baseball team through the Smyrna Baseball League, and my dad was one of the coaches. By the end of the season, two players from each team were picked for the All-Star team and my brother happened to be one of them. The All-Star game came around, and the players were having a blast chatting and just being kids. About midway into the game, several of the players were having a conversation, and my brother asked the question: "Who do you support—Trump or Biden?" A few of the players accused my brother of racism for asking that question. Troubled, my brother ran up to my dad and explained that his teammates accused him of being racist for liking Trump. My dad responded, "Just go back and have fun playing with the boys. Leave it at that!" Mistakenly, both my dad and brother thought that was the end of it. Much to their dismay, it wasn't.

Silenced and Censored

Within a couple days, my dad received a text from the white coach saying that my brother had done something so egregious that the black coach threatened to leave the league unless my dad was punished. My dad ignored the text because he doesn't like playing fifth grade games. On the day of the draft, approximately three months later, my dad received a call from the president of the league. Apparently, my dad was being accused of racism and homophobia and would no longer be allowed to coach for the league. My dad asked the president what he said that could be characterized as racist or homophobic. The league president responded that he couldn't reveal the statements because that would disclose the identity of his accusers. Very kindly, my dad responded, "That's not how life works. You cannot just accuse somebody of something but not tell them what they allegedly said."

My dad went on to ask: "What is homophobia?"

The president replied, "I don't know. Maybe you should look it up in the dictionary. Many people have different definitions."

My father responded again, respectfully, "You are kicking me out for something you can't even define? You can't even define what homophobia is but you are kicking me out because of it?"

"The decision has already been made," the president retorted.

Midway through the phone call, my dad posed another question to the president: "Do you realize that you are discriminating against me and persecuting me because I am a Christian?"

The president laughed and said, "It has nothing to do with it."

"That is exactly what it is," my dad countered. "You are persecuting me because of my political and spiritual beliefs—accusing me of being racist with no evidence. You won't allow me to defend myself, and really what is happening is a 45-year-old black man and a 40-year-old white man are persecuting my 9-year-old son because he supports Donald Trump."

My dad and brother were mistreated for being conservative Christians. This is just one out of thousands of stories in America. I suspect many will accuse me of using racist terminology, but the facts are the facts. There was, in fact, a white and black liberal coach.

Our religious liberty is being stripped from us at an alarming rate! Perhaps this persecution has never landed at your door, and you've never been the direct target of discrimination. The days of your insulation are rapidly coming to an end! As American citizens, regardless of age, race, religion, or gender, it's our duty to defend the freedoms that our forefathers sacrificed their lives, fortunes, and honor to secure for us.

> "For to whom much is given,
> much shall be required."
> (Luke 12:48, RGT)

I want to end this chapter with a quote from Yuri Bezmenov, a former KGB informant and Soviet journalist who is known for exposing how the Soviet Union undermined Western societies. Yuri stated:

> Ideological subversion, or psychological warfare, or "active measures"—what it basically means is: to change the perception of reality of every American to such an extent that despite the abundance of information, no one is able to come to sensible conclusions in the interest of defending themselves, their families, their community, and their country. It's a great brainwashing process which goes very slow and is divided into four basic stages. The first one being demoralization. It takes from fifteen to twenty years to demoralize a nation... The result you can see... Most of the people who graduated in the sixties, drop-outs or half-baked intellectuals, are now occupying the positions of power in the government, civil service, business, mass media, and the educational system. You are stuck with them. You cannot get rid of them. They are contaminated. They are programmed to think and react to certain stimuli in a certain pattern. You cannot change their mind, even if you expose them to authentic information. (44)

Before I move on to the next chapter, I want to define Marxism. We often throw that term around without really having an idea of what it means. To put it simply, Marxism is a theory that ultimately leads to communism by separating society. All members of society are in one of two categories: the oppressed or the oppressor.

*** TAKE A *CHANCE!* ***

Choose a topic—like "The Pilgrims' Fight for Freedom," "Free Speech vs. Government Overreach," or "Silent Prayer with Loud Consequences"—and dive deep by completing a series of interactive activities. From creating social media posts to leading discussions in youth groups or debating with friends, design each activity to foster understanding, inspire action, and build confidence in speaking up for what matters.

"A well regulated Militia,
being necessary to the security of a free State,
the right of the people to keep and bear Arms,
shall not be infringed." (45)

—Second Amendment

Chapter 3
Shall Not Be Infringed

Our right to bear arms didn't begin in 1791 when the Second Amendment of the US Constitution was amended within the first ten amendments known as the Bill of Rights. The ideas within our Second Amendment began a long time before then. Even in the time of ancient Rome and Greece, the idea of defending oneself and one's family existed. A large majority of the Greeks and Romans even carried their own weapons to battle. However, it was the English that embodied ideas from Machiavelli. From the reign of Alfred the Great all the way to the English Civil War, very few changes were made to the English arms laws. There was no difference between the militia and the everyday citizen. Every man carried the same weapons, and they took honor in this freedom. "It was these citizen soldiers—not mercenary armies—that fought off the Vikings, the French, the Dutch, and the Spanish, that settled the New World, and that would one day found and fight for the United States of America. (46)

Within the United States Constitution, *the Declaration of Independence,* and the Bill of Rights are what can be known as natural rights/laws. In simple terms, this means that, regardless of the time or location, our rights will never change because they are based upon objective and moral truth. I don't typically obtain definitions from Wikipedia, but I like their definition of natural law as a "philosophy asserting that certain rights are inherent by virtue of human nature, endowed by nature—traditionally by God or a transcendent source—and that these can be understood universally through human reason. As determined by nature, the law of nature is implied to be objective and universal; it exists independently of human understanding, and of the positive law of a given state, political order, legislature or society at large." (47)

Our rights were neither created nor gifted to us by mankind; they are a gift from God Almighty. Thomas Aquinas wrote that, "By nature, all men are equal in liberty, but not in other endowments." (48) Our Founding Fathers recognized that America could only succeed if God's law was its cornerstone. Frédéric Bastiat said, "Life, liberty, and property do not exist because men have made laws. On the contrary, it was the fact that life, liberty, and property existed beforehand that caused men to make laws in the first place." (49)

The Second Amendment of the United States Constitution was not ratified so we could head to the firing range and have some target practice. While that is great, the Second Amendment was intended to assure that "We the People" can defend ourselves and our families from a tyrannical government. The last sentence of the Second Amendment states, "...the right of the people to keep and bear Arms, shall not be infringed." The government does not have the right or authority to interfere with our firearms. It is unconstitutional.

Our Second Amendment is continuously under attack, even by those we considered politically friendly. Power-loving politicians and activists are stripping us of our constitutional right to carry in the name of "safety" and "protecting others." Frankly, the only group of people who profit off the banning of guns, gun-free zones, and gun control as a whole are the criminals. According to the Crime Research Center, 94% of mass shootings since 1950 have occurred in gun-free zones. Many like to circulate the argument that "guns don't stop mass shootings." But what they don't divulge in those statistics is that when there is a gun, a law-abiding citizen typically shoots the criminal before the situation escalates and becomes a mass shooting. Where does nearly every single mass shooting occur? In gun-free zones. Criminals are cowards and prey on the weak.

Many of you are probably familiar with the Covenant School shooting in Nashville, TN, where Audrey Hale, a member of the rainbow cult, shot up a Christian private school. However, many of you are also probably aware of how long it took for the shooter's manifesto to be released. Actually, it was never released; it was accidentally leaked. But why? Why were our Tennessee politicians not demanding the release of this manifesto? Why were the police and courts not releasing it?

Every manifesto from these shootings should be released as soon as possible. "We the People" deserve the truth, and one of the ways you prevent more shootings is by informing citizens. With that being said, the public doesn't need to know the specific plans and details, but we deserve to know the shooter's motives and intentions.

THE INFRINGEMENT ON OUR RIGHT

Politicians, unelected bureaucrats, activists, and leaders across America are continuously advocating for gun control and the removal of our right to defend ourselves from a tyrannical government. I stumbled upon a quote from a writer by the name of Joshua Baker. In his book, *Deinfringe*, he stated:

> I use the term Anti-Self Defense Movement (ASDM): This encompasses anti-gun groups and persons looking for government control of firearms. Saying anti-gun does not quite relay their real position; they are, in fact, against self-defense. For example, England was "anti-gun," and when that didn't produce the correct result they became "anti-knife," and now some places are charging people for using pepper spray to defend themselves. When gun control doesn't work, they will add another item they want to control. (50)

It is no coincidence that these tyrants want to take away our right to carry and defend our families when you understand their chief goal: control. Throughout history, leaders and tyrants begin removing guns and other lines of defense from their people so they have no way of fighting back. From the research I've done, when I hear the term gun-control, I automatically hear Joseph Stalin, Mao Zedong, and other communist/socialist dictators throughout history who systematically took away their people's rights to defend and then attacked.

Joseph Stalin, the Soviet dictator responsible for the death of between five and eight million of his own people admitted, "If the opposition [to the Bolsheviks] disarms, all is well and good. If it refuses to disarm, we shall disarm it ourselves." (51) Tyrants have always first disarmed those they wished to rule and have power over. Mao Zedong, who came to power in China in 1949, uttered these words in a speech: "Political power grows out of the barrel of a gun. The Communist Party must hold the gun, and the gun must never be allowed to hold the Party." (52)

Before the twentieth century, there were gun laws in place, but they did not come close to what we call "gun control" today. The first official gun control bill was passed in the early 1930s called The National Firearms Act of 1934. This bill was the "solution" to combating the gang violence that had reached an all-time high during the Great Depression. Essentially, the NFA imposed a tax on firearms including shotguns, rifles, machine guns, mufflers, and silencers. In addition to that, this bill required registration of all "NFA firearms with the Secretary of the Treasury." (53) John Ross said:

> The National Firearms Act fit in perfectly with the systematic creation of government programs and deficit spending that Franklin Roosevelt immediately began to institute the instant he took office. The NFA was a model vehicle for the continued expansion of government power: It was arbitrary; it gave the government sweeping authority over something very common; it focused on inanimate objects rather than criminal behavior; it levied draconian taxes on these objects; and most certainly, it created millions of criminals with the stroke of a pen... (54)

The language surrounding this bill was convincing enough to most politicians and the general public, but it was just the beginning and a slippery slope leading to more egregious gun control. If you give them an inch, they will take a mile. Gun control laws rarely strike at the root of the problem—lawbreakers who commit crimes.

Today, the NFA is a hefty fifty-one pages, which makes law-abiding citizens out to be criminals due to the heavy restrictions. Fast-forward to 1968. After the assassination of RFK, the Gun Control Act (GCA) was enacted. Many have compared this law to the Nazi Firearms

Law because their handgun registration eventually led to confiscation and the restriction of firearm ownership to party members only. The bill that is referenced nearly every time there is a mass shooting is the Assault Weapon Ban of 1993. Everything within this bill is junk, and it's all propaganda. This may be of no surprise to you by now, but the term "assault weapon" actually came from Nazi Germany. Hitler wanted to provoke fear around the weapon. Very few military departments even refer to them as "assault weapons." The Air Force calls them "Aircrew Self-Defense Weapons." Homeland Security calls them "Personal Defense Weapons."

Everybody with a brain knows that punishing everyone because of one person's bad decision(s) is not a good idea. Security measures are one thing; banning guns is another. It is an example of government overreach that is neither constitutional nor effective. If bans were successful, shouldn't we be outlawing a myriad of things?

The National Research Council conducted a study in 2005 and published their findings: "A recent evaluation of the short-term effects of the 1994 federal assault weapons ban did not reveal any clear impacts on gun violence outcomes." (55) In 2004, the National Institute of Justice said, "There has been no discernable reduction in the lethality and injuriousness of gun violence, based on indicators like the percentage of gun crimes resulting in death or the share of gunfire incidents resulting in injury." (56)

Shall Not Be Infringed

Famous quotes from American politicians, leaders, and activists calling for an infringement upon our right to bear arms:

"Yes, people pull the trigger, but guns are the instrument of death. Gun control is necessary, and delay means more death and horror."
—Eliot Spitzer (2012)

"The fact of the matter is that there is no legitimate use for these [assault] weapons."
—Chuck Schumer (2003)

"We cannot have assault weapons in our society… They need to be banned… military-grade assault weapons, those just don't belong in the hands of everyday people."
—Bill de Blasio (2019)

"Banning guns addresses a fundamental right of all Americans to feel safe."
—Diane Feinstein (1993)

"I don't care if you want to hunt, I don't care if you think it's your right. I say 'Sorry, it's 1999.' We have had enough as a nation. You are not

allowed to own a gun, and if you do own a gun,
I think you should go to prison."
—Rosie O'Donnell (1999)

Regardless of these activists' philosophies, gun control does not work and is diametrically opposed to the rights afforded to us within our Constitution. Kansas City's chief of police concurred, "Criminals acquire guns by theft, by trade, or by using legal surrogate buyers. Drug dealers do not purchase their guns over the counter." (57) Willis Ross from the Florida Police Chiefs Association stated, "I think any working policeman will tell you that the crooks already have guns. If a criminal fills out an application and sends his application… he's the biggest, dumbest crook I've ever seen." (58)

In the words of Thomas Jefferson, "Laws that forbid the carrying of arms… disarm only those who are neither inclined nor determined to commit crimes. Such laws make things worse for the assaulted and better for the assailants; they serve rather to encourage than prevent homicides, for an unarmed man may be attacked with greater confidence than an armed one." (59)

Red Flag Laws

Red flag laws permit the temporary seizure of a weapon from a person deemed a threat by law enforcement. They have frequently been called "common sense" laws by many (including Republicans) after mass shootings occur. Shortly after the Covenant School shooting in Nashville, TN, the Governor of Tennessee, Bill Lee, proposed red flag laws. They are 100% unconstitutional because they allow "courts to prevent people who show signs of being a danger to themselves or to others from having access to firearms (as by ordering the seizure of weapons)." (60) Instead of addressing the root cause of criminal activity, politicians pretend that guns are living beings with a will of their own and mistakenly strip law-abiding citizens of their God-given right to defend their families from a tyrannical government. In truth, no gun has ever made a conscious decision to harm a human being. It cannot.

Instead of faulting inanimate objects, I believe we should and must go to the root of the problem. In my personal opinion, I believe the root of this issue is the educational system indoctrinating our children with "woke" ideologies. In the Covenant School shooting manifesto, Aubrey (the shooter) said, "Wanna kill all you little cr*ckers, bunch of faggots with your white [privileges], f**k you faggots..." (61) This shooter believed that all white people are born racist and with white privilege. But where did this hate stem from? From the educational system indoctrinating children with critical race theory. In an X tweet, Congresswoman Majorie Taylor Green said this, and I couldn't agree more: "Every shooter's manifesto should be public. There is absolutely no reason to hide this. Unless, of course, our government wants to hide the fact that these shooters are on SSRIs and usually brainwashed by leftist's propaganda." (62)

Red flag laws are strengthened by the notion that if someone poses a threat, the state can confiscate their arms. But what's stopping them from taking the right to bear arms away from "right-wing extremists" because they said something they deem hateful or "bigoted" that someone just simply didn't like? New York State Senator Kevin Parker introduced a bill mandating that any gun-owner applicants have their social media accounts reviewed before receiving the permit. Within the proposed legislation, law enforcement officials were encouraged to investigate "commonly known profane slurs used or biased language used to describe race, national origin, ancestry, gender, religion, disability or sexual orientation; threatening health or safety of another person, or an act of terrorism." (63) Essentially, if someone made a comment on social media that wasn't "politically correct," they were at risk of not being able to receive a handgun permit.

Similar to red flag laws, "social credit scores" utilized in China punish infractions like bad driving, buying too many video games, posting controversial content on social media, or wasting money on frivolous purchases. If your "social credit score" is too low, your travel may be restricted until you perform enough "good deeds." It may sound dystopian, but I can assure you that this cultural

Marxism is already at work in America. Police can confiscate or prevent you from passing background checks if your social media accounts don't meet their criteria.

There are too many arguments in favor of gun control to count. The logical discrepancy with gun control laws is that they assume criminals obtain guns through the legal process; however, more often than not, they are stolen or purchased off the record. Undeniably, guns are not the problem. We do not have a gun problem; we have a lack of morality in society. We have a people problem. Guns don't kill people. Knives don't kill people. Cars don't kill people. People kill people. This is a psychological, social, societal problem—not a gun problem. This should not be a complex idea. Unfortunately, it has morphed into one.

We can almost always expect the media to turn mass shootings into a relentless push for gun control. "We the People" have to say *enough*. Until we address the root of the problem, mass shootings will continue and the bandwagoning for the confiscation of guns will carry on. Gun control and red flag laws do not work because they strip law-abiding citizens of their God-given right to defend themselves and their families from a tyrannical government. We must maintain our Second Amendment rights.

*** TAKE A *CHANCE!* ***

Explore and defend your Second Amendment rights,

applying what you've learned through practical steps. Begin by understanding the historical context of the right to bear arms, viewing it as both a natural law and a safeguard against government overreach. You can research current gun laws and proposals to see how these measures may impact constitutional rights, discuss gun-free zones' effectiveness with friends, and participate in mock debates on controversial policies like red flag laws. By presenting historical cases and the original intent behind the Second Amendment, you can better understand and articulate the role of self-defense in American freedom.

"He who controls the language
controls the masses." (64)

—Saul Ailinski
Author of *Rules for Radicals*

Chapter 4
The Digital Age

The left has successfully used the media to create racial tension between blacks and whites, to distort male and female roles in society, and to essentially divide and conquer a country.

In 2007, the World Economic Forum published a video of Klaus Schwab, a German economist and founder of the WEF, showing their headquarters and explaining what they do. During the clip, Schwab said something that should not be overlooked:

> If we look at our stakeholders, we have businesses, of course, as a very important audience, we have politics, we have continuous partnerships with many governments around the world, and, of course, NGO's (non-government organizations). We have trade unions, we have all the different types of music, of course, very important experts and scientists, academia. Because if we are looking at the future, I think we should look at new solutions, and the new solutions will be very much driven by technological developments, religious leaders, and we have social entrepre-

neurs. (65)

The advancements of technology have been both a blessing and a curse to society. Only in recent history has it been possible to make instant contact with someone internationally. Because of the cell phone, we are now able to connect with family and friends from a distance. This is a tremendous blessing to servicemen abroad, traveling businessmen and women, and grandparents longing to see their grandchildren.

Social Media

Through the release of the cell phone into the world of technology, social media has become one of the hottest commodities, allowing people to become completely disconnected from reality and the present moment. This is the most hyper-connected age in human history. Ever since the smartphone was introduced, anxiety, depression, suicide, sleep deprivation, etc., have been completely off the charts.

This obviously has a great effect on society as a whole, but specifically the younger generations. According to Common Sense Media, Generation Z spends an astounding nine hours per day consuming a slew of different types of online media entertainment. (66) This is greatly affecting relationships and the way teens and children interact with others. A recent survey conducted by the Pew Research Center found that nearly 35% of twelve to seventeen-year-olds admit that they rarely have face-to-face interactions with their peers and friends. (67) The survey also revealed that 63% of the teens relied on texting for the primary form of communication between peers and friends. (68) Social media has also created an entire desensitized generation.

Both kids and adults are being bombarded with an unrealistic fairytale world through social media. Need sexual gratification? Pleasure yourself with porn. Need fellowship? Feeling lonely? Hop onto a social media platform to feel fulfilled. In reality, it's all a big sham. Social media and online entertainment is only making the epidemics of loneliness, depression, and anxiety worse. A study conducted by *The Journal of Preventive Medicine* showed that the more time that people spend on social media, the more lonely they feel in their everyday lives. (69)

Nearly 95% of teens ages twelve through seventeen are online, accessing sites such as YouTube, Instagram, Facebook, Tiktok, Omegle, Whisper, Snapchat, Reddit, etc. The Pew Research Center says that nine out of ten teenagers play video games. (70) Many can find limited enjoyment through these social media apps, and there are positives that can come from them. However, countless studies have shown correlation between the rise in mental health problems and the increased use of social media. Through the cell phone and social media, we have created a bridge that connects families continents apart, but, ironically, family units have never been more distant. Teenagers cannot converse with someone sitting across the table from them; they hide behind their devices. This generation hungers for instant gratification, endless immediate entertainment, and sex on demand, yet their hunger is never satisfied. Gen Z is dying inside.

COVID-19 pulled back the curtains and exposed the concerning condition of teens hooked on social media and the bait predators use to lure them. During the pandemic, predators took advantage of the skyrocketing amount of time children and teens were on social media. Wherever you find children or teens, you can be assured that's where you'll find predators. It also revealed that humans were not created to be separated. We were created by God to require touch, personal fellowship, and communion with others.

Omegle

A particular site where predators were taking advantage of children was Omegle. Robby Starbuck and Landon Starbuck, who are warriors for freedom in the state of Tennessee and across the country, released a short documentary film that they had been working on for quite some time on the Omegle app. This short documentary was released in late 2023. Just days before the film's release, the app had been shut down by the owner due to the heavy amount of lawsuits he was getting.

Essentially, Omegle was an American-run app with the slogan: "A place to meet strangers." For nearly a decade, this app was allowing grown men to log on and offer explicit, inappropriate content for children. While this app has been removed, there are many other social media apps making this filth accessible to our vulnerable children and young adults today.

For apps like Instagram or Snapchat, men will create accounts posing as a young girl or boy with a fake profile picture. After gaining the teen's confidence, they will reach out asking to get to know them and meet either over the phone or in person. Unfortunately, many times the predator is able to convince the teen to send inappropriate pictures, exploiting them later on Pornhub and other sites.

In 2015, a YouTuber by the name of Coby Persin filmed a video called "The Dangers of Social Media (Child Predator Social Experiment)." In his experiment, Persin "... created a fake Facebook profile for one 15-year-old 'Jason Biazzo' and then, with the parents' permission, contacted the three unsuspecting teenage girls to see how far they would go to meet their new online contact. (71) His video is extremely telling and a testament to how convinced these young girls can be that they are speaking with someone their age. Persin's video has been viewed over sixty-three million times on YouTube.

Pornography

Sadly, the average age of someone first encountering pornography is age eleven. (72) According to *CyberPsychology and Behavior,* by age eighteen, approximately 93% of young boys and 62% of girls have consumed pornography of some type online. One click leads to another, and BOOM, you are on a porn site. This is how Big Tech and the porn industry make bank off of you and your children.

Pornography is one of the key components of child sex trafficking. Not only are underage minors viewing this harmful and sexual content, but many underage girls are featured and exploited all across the internet. In 2020, *The New York Times* published an article titled: "The Children of Pornhub." The article detailed young teens who were mocked, humiliated, and exploited by them. One of the young girls told the writer, "They made money off my pain and suffering." Another woman told him, "Pornhub became my trafficker." Nearly every single teen listed in the article who was exploited through Pornhub has either attempted or committed suicide. Nicholas Kristof, the writer, began the article by stating:

> Pornhub prides itself on being the cheery, winking face of naughty, the website that buys a billboard in Times Square and provides snow plows to clear Boston streets. It donates to organizations fighting for racial equality

and offers steamy content free to get people through COVID-19 shutdowns. That supposedly "wholesome Pornhub" attracts 3.5 billion visits a month, more than Netflix, Yahoo, or Amazon. Pornhub rakes in money from almost three billion ad impressions a day. One ranking lists Pornhub as the 10th-most-visited website in the world. Yet there's another side of the company: Its site is infested with rape videos. It monetizes child rapes, revenge pornography, spy cam videos of women showering, racist, misogynist content, and footage of women being asphyxiated in plastic bags. A search for "girlsunder18" (no space) or "14yo" leads in each case to more than 100,000 videos. Most aren't children being assaulted, but too many are. (73)

Pornhub released a statement saying, "Pornhub is unequivocally committed to combating child sexual abuse material, and has instituted a comprehensive, industry-leading trust and safety policy to identify and eradicate illegal material from our community. (74) But, of course, that is not what the evidence is showing.

Later in the article, Kristof adds:

> The problem goes far beyond one company. Indeed, a rival of Pornhub, XVideos, which arguably has even fewer scruples, may attract more visitors. Depictions of child abuse also appear on mainstream sites like Twitter, Reddit, and Facebook. And Google supports

the business models of companies that thrive on child molestation. Google returns 920 million videos on a search for "young porn." Top hits include a video of a naked "very young teen" engaging in sex acts on XVideo along with a video on Pornhub whose title is unprintable here. (75)

Reports showed that in 2015, there were nearly 6.5 million files/videos, in 2017 it was up to 20.6 million, and in 2019, a striking 69.2 million. (76)

Shortly after "The Children of Pornhub" article was released, the senior VP and executive director for the National Center on Sexual Exploitation, Dawn Hawkins, responded and called for the shutdown of Pornhub as a whole. He wrote:

> We celebrate that many victims of pornography have brought some measure of change to the hard-core pornography industry as a result of Mr. Kristof's investigation. But we cannot wrap a pretty bow around this story. Pornhub's "improvements" will not stop the scourge of vile content it profits from. Pornhub's 13 million existing videos depicting content ranging from rape, child sexual abuse, incest, and misogynistic and racist themes—to name a few—garner hundreds of thousands of views, and each view will make Pornhub only more money. It can't just make changes going forward; all existing videos must be removed. Facilitat-

ing the distribution of child sexual abuse material and profiting from it is an abhorrent act and enough on its own to merit Pornhub's shutdown. None of Pornhub's changes solve the inherent trauma experienced by individuals in pornography, or those who have been victimized against their will, and they don't solve the nature of Pornhub itself: a company built on the exploitation of men, women and, yes, children. Pornhub cannot be fixed with a few tweaks; it must be shut down completely. True justice for survivors demands nothing less. (77)

A more recent investigation into Pornhub was conducted by an investigative journalist by the name of Arden Young. Arden began her investigation into Pornhub in February of 2023. Shortly after she released her exposé, I had the honor of interviewing her on my show. During the interview, she noted that she was able to speak with around a dozen Pornhub employees.

Arden stated that it wasn't hard to find information and get questions answered. On one occasion, she called their advertising company named Traffic Junkie. Posing as an advertiser, she hunted for details by asking questions such as: "I am an advertiser, and I have videos of this girl who looks super young. If she turns out to be underage, what happens?" Arden said that multiple employees told her and another journalist, "Your account will not be suspended, and we will not report to law enforcement." So essentially, an advertiser can submit videos, including underage girls being raped, and nothing will be done about it because they can't "verify." She added that the employees offered additional information: "What we deem underage is what we deem underage. We have our own criteria, and if we deem someone underage in your video, we won't suspend your account, and we do not report to law enforcement."

In her exposé, Arden spoke with the Pornhub executive, Mike Farley, who made some disturbing and telling comments—not the kind you would expect an executive employee at Pornhub to reveal. Arden emphasized that in both of her meetings with Farley, he detailed a loophole where the content moderation team couldn't possibly verify whether or not the faces submitted actually matched up to a body, considering that most porn videos do not reveal the faces of those in the videos. Arden stated, "He's talking about how this is something that rapists [and] traffickers could exploit to make money. He is absolutely sure that underage videos are up there and it is just something they shrug their shoulders and say, 'Well, shut up about it...' So this is something they are very aware of."

Arden later stated:

> Mike Farley essentially tells me that porn is addictive; it is a drug. We don't know the health or societal implications... It can't be normal, it can't be healthy. And

funny enough, he really aligns his viewpoint of pornography with Jordan Peterson's view on pornography, which is that it's damaging to relationships, it is not normal for the average male to have a thousand naked women at his fingertips at any given time of the day, it is just not a normal human experience. Those were really the questions and opinions that Mike Farley was posing, which was really surprising to me since he has been in the adult industry for eleven years now and is pretty high up in the company and is the product manager over Pornhub.

Arden added despondently, "His justifier for all of it was, 'it makes a lot of money.'"
Even top employees at Pornhub understand that pornography is unhealthy, it is addictive, and it rewires our brains. The devastating impact that pornography has had on children, marriages, and families is catastrophic. The traditional family with a masculine father, a nurturing mother, and happy children has nearly been erased. Our depraved society, lusting like rabid animals, has a broken, distorted view of God's original design for sex, and we have traded the beautiful for the boorish. Young adults seeking lifelong partners to build a godly family often approach relationships with understandable caution, as the modern dating scene can feel like a cesspool. What can we do to preserve our children's innocence, to protect marriages, and to safeguard people from the ruin-

ous harms of pornography? There are plenty of apps and browser protection systems that can prevent inappropriate content from popping up. For young kids, I would suggest not giving them a smart phone until a certain age and especially not social media until they are mature enough to responsibly use the apps.

We must make porn harder to access through third-party identification. For several years, many considered the porn industry nearly impossible to regulate and restrict. On June 15, 2022, a newly elected representative from the state of Louisiana, Rep. Laurie Schlegel, introduced a bill that is making a big difference in the porn industry. This was the first bill of its kind to ever be introduced, but it was not the last. States including Arkansas, Montana, Mississippi, Utah, Virginia, and Texas have also passed a similar age-identification law in order to access pornography. Many other activists and legislators are working on other states also. Here is an excerpt from the bill:

> Pornography is creating a public health crisis and having a corroding influence on minors. Due to advances in technology, the universal availability of the internet, and limited age verification requirements, minors are exposed to pornography earlier in age. Pornography contributes to the hyper-sexualization of teens and prepubescent children and may lead to low self-esteem, body image disorders, an increase in problematic sexual activity at younger ages, and increased desire

among adolescents to engage in risky sexual behavior. Pornography may also impact brain development and functioning, contribute to emotional and medical illnesses, shape deviant sexual arousal, and lead to difficulty in forming or maintaining positive, intimate relationships, as well as promoting problematic or harmful sexual behaviors and addiction. (78)

This bill holds the porn sites liable unless the websites require the users to show their government ID (proving they are at least eighteen or older). Since this bill has been passed, according to reports from the Ethical Capital Partners, Pornhub's site traffic in Louisiana has dropped 80%. (79) The bill was "hurting" their business, so Pornhub claimed it was an infringement on their freedom of expression. Several lawsuits have been filed by the Free Speech Coalition, the pornography industry's trade association, against these age-identification bills. I would submit to you all that preventing children from being able to view and be showcased in sexually explicit content is not an infringement upon our First Amendment. Rather, it is called protecting children's innocence. This is a money-grab. Pornhub and other sites do not care about protecting children. They care about making money.

Statistics have shown that Pornhub gets more global views than sites like Netflix and Amazon. According to Pornhub's 2018 in Review, there were over 33.5 billion visits in 2018 alone, equalling around 92 million daily visits (Pornhub, 2018). In 2019, it shot up to approximately 42 billion total visits, which totals nearly 115 million visits per day.

According to a recent article by *Politico*, "Pornhub did something else even more unprecedented." In three other states that passed similar bills (Utah, Mississippi, and Virginia), "It simply stopped operating. Users in these states who attempt to visit the site are greeted with a safe-for-work video of Cherie DeVille (a porn star), clothed, explaining the site's decision to pull out of the state." (80) This is there to get back at the state and retaliate for making porn more inaccessible. Pornhub's hope was that enough porn viewers would get angry at the state and complain.

As I have done more and more research on just this one bill, I can attest to the fact that change will happen when we take action. Christians must stop being silent and thinking we can't or won't make a difference. You can, and you will. Here's a prime example. Although she's a woke and left-leaning pop star, Billie Eilish made a statement on the Howard Stern Show in 2021 that should not be overlooked. Eilish admitted, "I used to watch a lot of porn, to be honest. I started watching porn when I was like eleven... I think it really destroyed my brain, and I feel incredibly devastated that I was exposed to so much porn." (81) It takes influencers to create change. How can you use the influence God has given you?

Holding Big Tech Accountable— Going Forward

This is where "We the People" have to rise up and pressure our legislators. Big Tech companies like Netflix Inc., Google, Apple, and others have absolutely zero incentive to protect children. There are no laws standing in the way of Big Tech companies and their untapped ability to block predators from reaching your innocent children. Sadly, they could help, but they simply lack incentive to prevent these predators from getting to your children. It's no coincidence that many of the founders of these large Big Tech companies have their hands in the World Economic Forum (WEF), World Health Organization (WHO), the United Nations (UN), and more. It is all a part of the 2030 Agenda and a one-world government where "We the People" are slaves and peasants to the elitists. Big Tech is run by politicians, and many Big Tech companies fund our politicians.

Regardless of the negligence of Big Tech companies, self-governed adults must not abdicate their responsibilities as parents. You must assume that no one is going to protect your children but you. Be wise! God expects you to safeguard, teach, and train your own children. They are not the responsibility of the state, though the state happily encroaches upon your family government every chance they get. The next generation is not comprised of lemmings who march to the indoctrinating orders of the public education system. If you utilize public education, you must pay attention to what your children are learning—even in kindergarten. Children are not widgets for the world's use. Their innocence must be protected, their minds must be nourished, and their souls must be trained to love and uphold a biblical worldview. Set them up for success. Limit their access to the web. Keep them away from social media. The biggest change factor is us.

Before moving on from this chapter, I don't want you to miss this. Some people, specifically feminists, have actually purported that the sex industry is a form of sexual liberation or freedom—even sexual "empowerment" for women. If we want to talk about women being oppressed in America, let's talk about the fact that the commercial sex industry consists of about 98% women and children, whereas those purchasing and viewing are nearly 99% men. The patriarchy is not oppressive. What's crushing and degrading is women being objectified and turned into hollowed-out shells, used and abused by a perverse industry that ultimately cares about satisfying primal lusts and making money. By sleeping around with multiple men, young girls and women are not living their best lives, nor are they liberated or empowered. They are stripped of dignity, and someone's innocent little girl, who once had hopes of finding a man to love and cherish her, is wounded and broken. In some cases, the damage is irreparable. Is this considered "liberation" by the feminist movement? Keeping men as docile as possible is the goal by the elitists. We have become a debased and desensitized society. We need the biblical definition of manliness now more than ever.

*** TAKE A *CHANCE!* ***

Examine how media messaging shapes public opinion, especially regarding cultural and political issues, and share your insights through social media or discussions. You can track your screen time to gauge its impact on your own mental health, experiment with a temporary social media fast, and reflect on the balance between online and real-world connections.

"God created man in His own image,
in the image of God He created him; male and
female He created them. God blessed them; and
God said to them, 'Be fruitful and multiply, and fill
the earth, and subdue it; and rule over the fish of the
sea and over the birds of the sky and over every
living thing that moves on the earth.'"

—Genesis 1:27-28, NASB

Chapter 5
The Poison of Gender Ideology

The topic of gender ideology alone could be made into a series of books because of how much it has ruined and impacted our entire culture. It has infiltrated advertisements, commercials, movies, and conversations. However, for the sake of this book, I have decided to focus my efforts on what has been dealt the greatest blow.

Out of all the research or books I've read, the most telling and educational of them all was the documentary, *What is a Woman?*, by Matt Walsh. (82) If you have not seen this yet, you must watch it immediately. This eye-opening film not only masterfully reveals how duped we are as a society overall, but it also exposes the woeful, half-witted ideologies hiding away in the minds of the majority of our college professors and medical professionals. And we trust these people to educate our children and provide our health care? After months and months of Matt traveling the country asking the top experts the simple question--"What is a woman?"--not a single expert could answer the question.

The History of Gender Ideology

There is debate from both sides of the aisle about where gender ideology truly began, but from the research I have conducted, I believe it really began with a homosexual German physician, Magnus Hirschfeld. After graduating from medical school, Hirschfeld founded the world's first LGBTQ rights organization called the Scientific-Humanitarian Committee in 1897. (83) He was labeled Germany's "Einstein of Sex." In 1919, he founded the Institute for Sexual Research wherein he provided resources, counseling, and advocated for policy changes. An article published by *The Times of Israel* stated, "Deeply troubled by the suicides among his LGBTQ patients, [Hirschfeld] set out to prove that queerness occurs naturally and should not be illegal." (84) He introduced the idea that those attracted to the same sex are "born that way." In 1928, Hirschfeld founded his last organization named the World League for Sexual Reform. (85) Known for coining new terms such as "transvestism," he brought the idea of a "third sex" and placed hermaphrodites, homosexuals, and transvestites in that category. (86)

In 1933, Hitler assumed power over Germany, which led to the destruction of Hirschfeld's institute. Two years later in 1935, Magnus Hirschfeld died in Nice, France. Hirschfeld's work was just the beginning of what is now known as gender ideology.

After Herschfeld's death, Germany produced another

sexologist by the name of Harry Benjamin. In 1966, he wrote the book titled *The Transexual Phenomenon*, which detailed his belief that an individual can medically change their gender.

Alfred Kinsey, another sexologist, founded the Institute for Sex Research at Indiana University in 1947, and boy, did he have a sickening agenda to change society completely. Dr. Miriam Grossman spoke about Kinsey in Walsh's documentary: "He wanted to rid society of Judeo-Christian values when it came to sexuality, and he worked very hard to do that. And I would say he succeeded. (87)

Kinsey held fast to the idea that all people, whether infantile or elderly, are sexual beings; therefore, we should affirm children's sexual desires. Although Kinsey's beliefs were fundamentally opposed to a biblical worldview, even he demonstrated some common sense when it came to the topic of "sex changes." Kinsey stated, "A male cannot be transformed into a female through any known surgical means. In other words, it would be very hopeless to attempt to amputate your male organs and implant a vagina." (88)

Many other misguided sexologists came and went, but the man responsible for releasing the floodgates of filth was John Money. His dark ideology, like an unstoppable river, has pulled every facet of our society into its powerful current. Historically, the terms "gender" and "sex" have been interchangeable terms. However, Money was the first person to introduce the notion that they are different, coining the term "gender role." His goal was to normalize sexual behavior regardless of age. Nonetheless, John Money is more widely known for firmly advocating what he called "sex change operations," and what I call genital mutilation surgery. Money became well acquainted with John Hopkins, and in 1965, Money's team of doctors performed the first genital surgery on a man by the name of Avon Wilson. In 1966, Money teamed up with others to found the John Hopkins Gender Identity Clinic. (89) Over the next few years, news started to pick up on what was happening at John Hopkins, which led to thousands of requests for these surgeries. (90)

Matt Walsh elaborates in detail on John Money and his most striking case with the Reimer twins in his book, *What is a Woman?* To simplify, this case included two healthy twin boys that were circumcised at eight days old. Unfortunately, there was a machinery malfunction while circumcising the first twin which burned his penis off. The parents were devastated and were unsure what to do. Shortly after, in 1967, the parents looked for help from John Money. "He stated that being raised as a female was in Reimer's interest and recommended sexual reassignment surgery." (91)

The parents took Money's advice and decided to raise their son as a girl, completing the necessary surgeries. John Money's team of physicians removed the son's damaged male genitalia and constructed female genitalia.

The family continued to affirm their son as a girl until he was in his teen years. Once the family finally told their son (whom they had affirmed as Brenda) that he was actually a boy, he decided to break free from the bondage they had kept him in and live his life as the man he was created to be. Reimer changed his name to David, began taking testosterone, and removed the female appendage to restore his male genitalia as best as possible.

Phil Gaetano wrote: "In his early twenties, Reimer attempted to commit suicide twice. According to Reimer, his adult family life was strained by marital problems and employment difficulty. Reimer's brother, who suffered from depression and schizophrenia, died from an antidepressant drug overdose in July of 2002. On 2 May 2004, Reimer's wife told him that she wanted a divorce. Two days later, at the age of thirty-eight, Reimer committed suicide by firearm." (92) All of this pain and the confusion he experienced as a child was the result of a lie spawned by sexual perversion. In my personal opinion, this case was all an experiment to satisfy John Money's sexual perversion. Regrettably, it has cost people their lives. John Money and the case of the Reimer twins was just the beginning of the damnable deluge now called gender ideology.

OUR SO-CALLED MEDICAL PROFESSIONALS

To be frank, I really had no idea what was happening

with the transgender issue and how openly the medical industry was pushing it until it landed on my family's doorstep. On August 6, 2022, my sister, who was seven years old at the time, was paralyzed in a freak swimming accident from the chest down. Because of her injury, we were placed in six different medical facilities in three separate states. During our eight-month time in these facilities, my family and I were able to see up close and personal how the rainbow cult was so heavily being pushed onto the children. Every single day we were bombarded by imagery promoting the rainbow cult. There were signs around the facilities, and the doctors and nurses would come in with stickers and pins promoting their preferred pronouns.

I recall one doctor's appointment where we sat down to meet the pediatrician. The student in residency had a large pin that said, "My Pronouns are They/Them." My initial thought was, *Wait a second, this person is going to give parents medical advice for their children but can't even tell me if they are a male or female. She has lied to herself and is mentally insane.*

We've reached a point where society is elevating individuals with psychological struggles to leadership roles just because it's trendy. Would anyone feel safe with a mentally unstable doctor in charge of their health? How can someone unsure of their own identity offer sound medical advice? As a Christian, would you trust a doctor who believes in a multitude of genders to care for your

Last Chance

children?

During this difficult season in the life of my family, we began to see conservative influencers and politicians exposing what these doctors were doing to minors—performing genital mutilation surgeries. I knew as a fifteen-year-old that I couldn't sit back and wait for someone else to act, so I prayed for a week or two asking the Lord what He wanted me to do. It was totally a God thing when Nicole with TPUSA Faith (a branch of Turning Point USA) reached out asking for my thoughts on a pro-life rally. That's when I felt the Lord calling me to host the first Teens Against Gender Mutilation rally. On January 28, 2023, with the help of Nicole and TPUSA Faith, I held the first Teens Against Gender Mutilation rally in Murfreesboro, TN. There were two things that surprised me the most during the promotional stage of this rally. First of all, the amount of people who didn't believe that these surgeries and hormones were being prescribed to minors was shocking. Secondly, I was stunned at the cowardice of the Christian community.

I remember one of the first radio shows I went on to advertise the event. The radio host literally didn't believe the stories I was sharing with him. He suggested that I was spreading misinformation and claimed I was brainwashed. I love it when people call me "brainwashed" because my response is always, "Well, at least my brain is clean."

The second thing that shocked me was how cowardly Christians and local churches have become. I naively thought this was a topic we could easily get churches to support in solidarity. Boy, was I wrong. I couldn't find one church in my area to boldly stand up for biblical truth at this rally. The issue of transgenderism has, unfortunately, been deemed too "controversial or political" to bring up in the church. Nothing could be further from the truth.

Educating children and parents of the emotional and physiological dangers that follow after making life-altering and irreversible decisions (such as cutting off your healthy breasts and genitals) isn't controversial. It is common sense. We are spiritual beings who were created to honor and worship our Creator, God Almighty. The act of mutilating our bodies is spiritual; it's an attack on the body God has made in His image and likeness. God did not make a mistake when he created us.

> "For You created my innermost parts; You wove me in my mother's womb. I will give thanks to You, because I am awesomely and wonderfully made; Wonderful are Your works, And my soul knows it very well. My frame was not hidden from You. When I was made in secret, And skillfully formed in the depths of the earth; Your eyes have seen my formless substance; And in Your book were written all the days that were ordained for me, When as yet there was not one of them." (Psalm 139:13-16, NASB)

Last Chance

Pastors and ministers, I urge you to speak boldly on these issues from your pulpits and social media platforms! It's time to prioritize eternal truth over tax-exempt statuses. In a world where belief in absolute truth is fading, we need to raise the unwavering standard of God's Word. Everything else is unstable ground! Expose the darkness of our culture, stand firm, and use your voice to protect the flock God has entrusted to you. People are trapped in delusion, and yet are desperate for truth. They wander aimlessly, searching for fulfillment in things like gender confusion, but these paths only lead to dissatisfaction and despair. Only God can fill that void.

True freedom and fulfillment come through speaking love and truth—the Gospel of Jesus Christ. Watered-down messages of tolerance and a permissive God only jeopardize souls, leading them away from eternal life. Be the voice in the wilderness, calling people to repent and return to the truth!

Despite the media's twisting of words and the counter-protests claiming it was an "anti-trans" rally, the goal of this event was to protect children's innocence. My first question in response to that allegation is: *How can you be against (anti) something that doesn't exist?* Of course, the people exist—nobody is denying that—but it is scientifically and biologically impossible to change your sex/gender. Even those who undergo these genital mutilation surgeries still have not changed their sex/gender. Not only does this ideology deny the natural laws of procreation and God's command in Genesis 1:28 to "go and multiply," it denies science, nature, reality, and just plain common sense.

Nonetheless, we had this rally out of complete love and compassion because the most loving thing you can tell someone is the truth. What's *not* loving and compassionate is to further someone's confusion by sending them down a path of destruction which encourages them to receive hormones and irreversible surgeries. Lies, no matter their popularity, are still lies. Our main speaker was Chloe Cole. At the time of our rally, she was an eighteen-year-old detransitioner going through horrible menopausal symptoms from what the medical industry had done to her. Around the age of twelve, she obtained an account on social media and started to compare herself to other women online. She didn't feel she looked like them. *Why don't I look like them? Is something wrong with me? Since I don't look like those women, would I be better off as a boy?* The voice in her head was unrelenting. After combing social media for some time, Chloe dove further into the abyss. Any remaining inhibitions were slowly deconstructed. She began viewing LGBTQ content from teens coming out as trans, gay, or lesbian, and she learned that she didn't have to be a girl. Confused by what she discovered on social media, Chloe began binding her breasts and seeing a therapist who diagnosed her with gender dysphoria. The medical professionals recommended that Chloe's parents provide her with cross-sex hormones, and if they didn't, she would be at risk for suicide. This fear tactic is commonly regurgitated by the medical industry: "Would you rather have a dead daughter or living son?" Basically, they scare parents into believing that if they don't allow their child to transition, then they will be at a high risk for committing suicide.

At age thirteen, Chloe's parents, under the direction of her therapist and the medical professionals, placed her on testosterone and puberty blockers. At age fifteen, she had a double mastectomy removing both of her healthy breasts. In an interview conducted by PragerU, Chloe stated, "I think reality really started to set in once I was in the post-op period and had to do my bandages/dressings and look down at what was left of my chest. It was really quite traumatizing… I suffered from complications from the surgery that I still suffer from to this day."

Later in the interview, Chloe lamented, "I realized what I had taken from myself and really my future children. I will no longer have the chance to breastfeed my children or bond with them in that way, and I don't know if I'll even be able to conceive a child… Pretty soon after, I realized I had regretted every step of my transition, and I wish that none of it had ever happened." (93) Chloe's story is heart-wrenching, especially considering the fact that her story is merely one out of thousands upon thousands.

The Poison of Gender Ideology

Do No Harm and the Extent of Genital Mutilation

Typically, in the first week of medical school, students are taught the Latin phrase: *Primum non nocere,* which is translated to, "First, do no harm!" (94) Additionally, upon graduating from medical school, you take the Hippocratic Oath. See the following:

1. I swear to fulfill, to the best of my ability and judgment, this covenant:

2. I will respect the hard-won scientific gains of those physicians in whose steps I walk, and gladly share such knowledge as is mine with those who are to follow.

3. I will apply, for the benefit of the sick, all measures [that] are required, avoiding those twin traps of overtreatment and therapeutic nihilism.

4. I will remember that there is art to medicine as well as science, and that warmth, sympathy, and understanding may outweigh the surgeon's knife or the chemist's drug.

5. I will not be ashamed to say "I know not," nor will I fail to call in my colleagues when the skills of another are needed for a patient's recovery.

6. I will respect the privacy of my patients, for their problems are not disclosed to me that the world may know. Most especially must I tread with care in matters of life and death. If it is given me to save a life, all thanks. But it may also be within my power to take a life; this awesome responsibility must be faced with great humbleness and awareness of my own frailty. Above all, I must not play at God.

7. I will remember that I do not treat a fever chart, a cancerous growth, but a sick human being, whose illness may affect the person's family and economic stability. My responsibility includes these related problems, if I am to care adequately for the sick.

8. I will prevent disease whenever I can, for prevention is preferable to cure.

9. I will remember that I remain a member of society, with special obligations to all my fellow human beings, those sound of mind and body as well as the infirm.

10. If I do not violate this oath, may I enjoy life and art, respected while I live and remembered with affection thereafter. May I always act so as to preserve the finest traditions of my calling and may I long experience the joy of healing those who seek my help.

The Poison of Gender Ideology

Hypothetically speaking, if I went to my primary care doctor and told him or her, "You know very well, Doc, that I've been struggling with depression and debilitating anxiety. I've contemplated this for months, and I've realized that if you removed my right arm then I wouldn't be anxious anymore, and I'd finally be happy. What I want you to do is cut my right arm off at my shoulder." Any sane doctor with common sense would first think that I need serious and immediate psychological help, but they would most likely respond professionally along the lines of, "Hannah, I cannot cut your arm off because, when I became a doctor, I took an oath to do no harm to any patient." Instead of our medical doctors actually helping children by telling them the truth--that you cannot change your sex--instead, they encourage them to seek hormone therapy and surgeries in an attempt to change who they were created to be. In doing so, they are abandoning their oath to "do no harm."

I submit to you that the doctors performing these surgeries and prescribing these medicines are just as clinically unstable as those seeking them. After a doctor diagnoses a child with gender dysphoria (which really isn't a diagnosis but an affirmation of the patients' feelings), they typically move forward with puberty blockers. One of the primary drugs that is prescribed to put a "pause on puberty" is called Lupron (Leuprolide). (95) This drug is FDA approved, and it is used to medically castrate children desiring to become the opposite gender. The same drug prescribed for our confused children was also used to castrate violent male sex offenders, halting their sexual desires. Medical professionals claim this drug is used to put a "pause or an offset" on puberty and that "there are no long-term effects." (96) However, Lupron—which was originally designed for sex offenders or men with prostate cancer—includes side effects like erectile dysfunction (ED), shrinkage of male genitalia, hot flashes, a reduction or absence in sexual desire, breast tenderness, and growth of breast tissue.

In an article published by The Federalist, Jane Robbins shares testimonials from individuals using Lupron: "Many of these patients have experienced extreme side effects that shattered their health and their lives, including severe joint pain, osteoporosis, compromised immune systems, and mental health issues such as severe depression and even suicidal ideation." (97) Again, these side effects stem from a drug the medical industry is prescribing and injecting into our physically healthy children.

There aren't many extensive research studies showing the long-term side effects of children diagnosed with gender dysphoria who were immediately placed on puberty blockers. However, when moving on from puberty blockers to cross-sex hormones, the risks and long-term effects become undeniably apparent.

A clinical trial conducted in 2011 revealed that 100% of the children placed on puberty blockers went on to receive cross-sex hormones. (98) After accepting cross-sex hormones, the most startling among a slew of side effects is infertility, which is typically guaranteed. Abigail Shirer, author of *Irreversible Damage*, wrote:

> Puberty is divided into five "Tanner stages," with Tanner stage 1 being no signs of puberty and 5 being full development of adult sexual organs. Puberty blockers are commonly administered as early as Tanner stage 2, when a girl is just starting to develop the first signs of breasts, her ovaries are still pre-fertile, and she has by definition not reached sexual maturity. When you halt a child at an early stage of puberty, her sexual organs freeze at that child-like state. If cross-sex hormones follow, there she will remain––incapable of biological reproduction or orgasm. (99)

But what if you change your mind? Can a young girl simply reset her body and return to her original state? Unfortunately, if a young girl decides she no longer wants to be a boy and stops taking testosterone (a cross-sex hormone), she is faced with permanent effects like a deepened voice and an enlarged clitoris. More extreme effects can be vaginal atrophy and bone/joint pain.

Let's talk about what they call "bottom surgery." Rarely do people undergoing reassignment surgery actually persist to the point of receiving "bottom surgery." This is largely due to the daunting success rate and the excruciating side effects.

Jane Robbins authored an online article for Public Discourse entitled, "The Cracks in the Edifice of Transgender Totalitarianism." In it, she stated:

> The [sex reassignment] surgery is gruesome. Female patients may be given hysterectomies, vaginectomies, and double mastectomies—all of the removed organs, of course, perfectly healthy—and some surgeons are stripping skin from girls' forearms to create non-functioning replicas of penises. Sex organs (penis, testicles, scrotum) of a male patient are removed, and a faux vagina is created that must be kept open with a dilator to prevent the wound from collapsing on itself and healing. (100)

Females desiring to become males undergo phalloplasty in order to create a penis-like structure. Men wishing to be female undergo vaginoplasty, which creates a vagina-like structure.

Where do we draw the line? How many children must face irreversible procedures like castration, mutilation, and sterilization before we wake up? In our scientifically advanced era, why do we cling to such twisted ideas and resist the wisdom that should guide us?

We've strayed from the path, normalizing behaviors that challenge the foundational principles of family and society. The acceptance of sex outside marriage led to the

The Poison of Gender Ideology

normalization of homosexuality, which in turn paved the way for legalizing gay marriage. Now, we find ourselves debating whether children should be allowed to undergo irreversible surgeries on healthy bodies. What comes next? Will we normalize pedophilia or bestiality?

This trajectory is the result of abandoning common moral standards and allowing our emotions to steer society toward destruction. Objective truth has been tossed aside, with the transgendered individual at the helm waving the flags of "they/them." Are we not paying attention? The dangers ahead are clear, yet many remain oblivious to the impending crash. Will those lost in this delusion ever wake up?

This discourse raises critical questions about our moral compass and the societal implications of our choices. It's essential to engage in these conversations thoughtfully and responsibly, considering the welfare of our children and the integrity of our society.

Many of you probably know our Secretary for "Health", Mr. Levine, who is obese and thinks he is a woman. Levine stated in mid-2023 that "gender-affirming care is medical care. Gender-affirming care is mental health care. Gender-affirming care is literally suicide prevention care. (101) Hmm. Interesting. According to the National Library of Medicine, "The suicide risk in transgender people is higher than the general population and seems to occur during every stage of transitioning." (102) Perhaps we should follow the science and listen to the statistics. Everything about the rainbow cult denies science and biological reality. It is all in defiance of Genesis 1:28.

Girls' Sports & Title IX

Title IX states, "No person in the United States shall, on the basis of sex, be excluded from participation in, be denied the benefits of, or be subjected to discrimination under any educational program or activity receiving Federal financial assistance." (103)

The sole purpose of Title IX was to offer women participating in sports the same opportunities as men and to prevent any further sex-based discrimination. Unfortunately, after years and years of hard work to give girls an equal playing field, we are now back to square one––except now we are fighting to get men removed from women's sports, women's bathrooms, locker rooms, shelters, safe spaces, and even prisons. The Democratic Party has bowed to the altar of political correctness and gender-bending, prizing it over speaking the truth and protecting women.

In early 2023, Representative Greg Stuebe reintroduced the Protection of Women and Girls in Sports Act of 2023, which prohibited men from competing in women's sports. (104) This was a common sense bill that you would think every congressional member could agree on, right? Nope! Every single Democrat voted against protecting women. They voted to allow men in women's sports and locker rooms.

The transgender ideology is not only ruining thousands upon thousands of innocent children's lives, it is also stripping countless girls of their innocence, dignity, and privacy. My siblings and I had a personal experience with this on June 18, 2023. We were swimming at a local community center in Murfreesboro. When we entered the women's locker room, we discovered, to our horror, a man (posing as a woman) undressing. For obvious reasons, we were uncomfortable changing in the presence of a man and quickly left.

One of the common phrases I hear from cross-dressing men is that "their rights are violated" because they cannot go to the girls' bathroom. Well, what about the rights of approximately 95% of women who do not want to undress or change their clothes with a man occupying the locker room or bathroom? It's awkward enough changing in front of the same gender! This invasion of privacy is happening to countless girls across the country.

Kylee Alons, the most decorated swimmer in North Carolina State's swimming program (31-time All-American, 5-time ACC champion, and 2-time NCAA champion), was forced to compete against male swimmer, Will Thomas, in the 100 freestyle. She has been impressively outspoken about being forced to share a locker room with a six foot four inches tall man with fully intact male genitalia. Because of the obvious uncomfortability, she ended up changing in the janitor's storage closet. Another swimmer, Paula Scanlan, who was Thomas's teammate at the University of Pennsylvania, was one of the few in the very beginning to speak out. Paula told me in an interview we had together that the University first came out with a warning: "If anyone speaks out against Lia swimming, you will regret it!" Then they used psychological fear tactics, "Lia swimming is non-negotiable, and we are here to offer services to make you ok with that." Scanlan, alongside other female teammates, was forced to see male genitalia as many as eighteen times per week. Additionally, the female swimmers were forced to change and expose themselves in front of a man up to eighteen times per week. The individuals that decried this were either completely dismissed or accused of bigotry. But Thomas is the real bigot, stealing girls' scholarships and titles and showing off his genitals to these girls. Stay in your lane, Thomas--literally!

In addition to stripping countless females of their innocence and dignity, the transgender ideology is physically harming them, too. Payton McNabb, a female high school volleyball player, was forced to compete against a man posing as a woman in a volleyball tournament. You may not realize this, but the men's volleyball net is seven inches higher than the women's because men statistically hit the ball harder than women. It's just a fact! Well, this male posing as a female spiked the volleyball at around seventy mph, striking Payton in the face and causing her to lie unconscious for over thirty seconds. To this day, Payton suffers from long-lasting--if not permanent--injuries like partial paralysis on her right side, vision problems, cognitive issues, anxiety/depression, and more. She needlessly suffers because we spit in the face of reality and prefer to placate people's feelings. This could have been avoided if we had simply followed the science that men cannot become women.

I have cataloged numerous accounts that represent the damaging consequences of gender ideology. Rather than cultivating our greatest resource and fertilizing the tender soil of their young hearts, we have planted wild thistles and thorn bushes that leave them wounded, helpless, and barren. But one intolerable repercussion has not yet been chronicled, and it should stir every breathing human with a pulse to action. Innocent girls are being raped due to transgender bathroom and locker room policies.

One story in particular is from October 2021 at a private academy in Rio Rancho, New Mexico. The mother of a young twelve-year-old found her daughter's diary that stated, "I was raped. I was raped. I was raped. F*cking kill me." After months of seeing a drastic mental health decline in her daughter, she finally found the reason behind it. The school, ASK Academy, had adopted gender ideology into the school and, to be more "inclusive," they allowed "gender-fluid" bathrooms. Allegedly, Ray (pseudonym of the young girl) was washing her hands as the male student walked over to her, grabbed and pinned her to the ground, ripped off her pants, and raped her. An article published by the Post Millennial stated: "Maggie (pseudonym) believes the main reason a male student was alone with her daughter that day, and had the opportunity to rape her, is because the school had fully embraced gender ideology. Upon reading through school documents and talking with her daughter and fellow parents, Maggie learned that, without her knowledge or consent, ASK Academy had fully embraced radical gender theory into its policies and classrooms." (105)

This story is just one horrific example of the result of adopting gender ideology. Truly, one of the most frightening issues of all is the fact that those who push back against this "woke" agenda and its policies are silenced or punished. A prime example was in Loudoun County, Virginia, on June 22, 2021, when Scott Smith was arrested at a school board meeting for "disorderly conduct." Scott Smith is the father of a fifteen-year-old female who was raped by a male student wearing a skirt on May 28, 2021. Right before the arrest, the Loudoun County Public School superintendent told those attending the meeting that the policy was misplaced due to the school system having no record of any assault ever occurring. According to an investigation done by the Daily Wire, right after that statement was made, "A woman wearing a rainbow heart shirt--a left-wing community activist--told Smith she did not believe his daughter, he says. His rage reached a boil, and he had a heated exchange of words with the woman. A police officer, there to keep the peace in the meeting, pulled on his arm. Smith yanked it away. Before he knew it, Smith says, he was hit in the face, handcuffed, and dragged across the floor, with his pants pulled down." (106) If not for Smith standing up and drawing attention to the assault, the police most likely would not have performed an investigation to build a case in order to arrest and prosecute the student that raped and assaulted these young girls.

At the 2024 Olympic Games, a female boxer was forced to compete against a male boxer. She quit forty-six seconds in because of how hard the male was punching her. If she hadn't forfeited, the male boxer could have killed her or severely wounded her. It is absolutely disgusting what we are allowing to happen. It used to be an unthinkable crime to punch and beat up women; now it's celebrated and defended.

Popular Arguments

"What about intersex or hermaphrodites?"
If you've ever debated a blue-haired liberal, you've more than likely heard them lean on the hermaphrodite or intersex argument to justify their flimsy belief in multiple genders or transgenderism as a whole. After getting into several debates myself on this topic, I decided to do some digging and get the facts. A recent study from the National Library of Medicine showed that the prevalence of intersex is about 0.018%. Intersex conditions that are ac-

counted for in the statistic can include but are not limited to: penile agenesis (male babies born without a penis), vaginal agenesis (female babies born without a vagina), Klinefelter Syndrome where male babies are born with an extra X chromosome (female), and Turner Syndrome where female babies are born with only one rather than two X chromosomes (female). These devastating cases should be treated case-by-case. However, using the intersex or hermaphrodite argument to justify children being pumped with hormones and having their healthy breasts and genitals cut off is a logical fallacy. It simply isn't honest.

"We just want to be accepted for who we really are!"

I get a lot of hate and backlash for bringing religion and God into the equation, specifically on the LGBTQ topic, but quite frankly, the LGBTQ rainbow movement is a religious cult. They worship their sin and sexual immorality. They have branded themselves as a "civil rights" issue, mistakenly claiming they were "born that way."

Humans are born different colors, but we are not born gay, lesbian, transgender, or heterosexual. Sexual immorality is a choice. Alleging that someone was born gay is like arguing that a married man who's cheating on his wife was born an adulterer. A husband who goes home to his wife and legitimately says, "Sorry, honey. I was just born this way," is unfaithful. As a free moral agent, he is responsible for his choices, and so are we all. I want to make it clear that this battle isn't heterosexual vs. rainbow-sexual. God demands holiness out of His people, and holiness is sex between a husband and a wife and abstinence until marriage.

You will hear many arguments similar to the two I listed disputed constantly by those on the left, but they use these attacks to draw attention away from the real issue. They are red herring fallacies.

THE TRUTH

The truth is that there are only two genders, and no one can change the sex God assigned them upon conception. Of course, we need God. We need our Savior, Jesus Christ. But even an irreligious man can follow the science and the data. If every man were gay, society would eventually end. If every woman were a lesbian, she would bear no children, and humanity would die off. This is common sense, and every society which upholds these moral standards enjoys a thriving civilization, much like how every family with covenant-keeping parents can enjoy a healthy home life where children flourish. The idea that we are even debating these topics reveals how debased and desensitized we have become.

The Bible makes it very clear that it is an abomination to God for a man to dress as a woman and for a woman to dress as a man: "A woman shall not wear a man's clothing, nor shall a man put on a woman's clothing; for whoever does these things is an abomination to the LORD your God." (Deuteronomy 22:5, NASB)

Oftentimes, you will hear people—even within the conservative movement—declare that what these confused individuals need is counseling. It may be true in some cases depending on the circumstances and trauma they have experienced, but, truly, no matter the amount of counseling sessions we sit through, the drugs we are prescribed, and the surgeries we undergo, the only way for anyone to experience true freedom is to submit to the infallible truth found only in the Word of God and to acknowledge his or her need of a Savior, Jesus Christ. It's the only way to revive a nation, the only way to preserve a family, and the only way to save an individual soul.

According to *The Washington Post,* approximately 21% of Generation Z identifies as LGBTQ, yet they are statistically the most depressed, suicidal, and anxiety-ridden generation. (107) This cannot be a coincidence when nearly every institution is imposing anti-scientific, anti-American, and frankly anti-Christian narratives down our throats. The intoxicating combination of social media and gender-fluidity is a dangerous and often fatal cocktail.

*** TAKE A *CHANCE!* ***

Watch Matt Walsh's What is a Woman?, *and discuss with a group the prevailing narratives of gender ideology.*

"Let divines and philosophers, statesmen and patriots, unite their endeavors to renovate the age by impressing the minds of men with the importance of educating their little boys and girls, inculcating in the minds of youth the fear and love of the Deity… And leading them in the study and practice of the exalted virtues of the Christian system." (108)

—Samuel Adams
Founding Father and Statesman

Chapter 6

Education

Thomas Jefferson spearheaded the idea of a public educational system funded by the taxpayers in America. However, his idea of a two-track system separating the laboring and the learned didn't come to fruition until the nineteenth century. Jefferson and our founders recognized that America's prosperity was dependent upon its citizens' understanding of where freedom originated--God Almighty.

Benjamin Franklin said, "A Bible and a newspaper in every house, a good school in every district--all studied and appreciated as they merit--are the principle support of virtue, morality, and civil liberty." (109) Early American education was centered around biblical principles and the concept of morality. The beginning of education in America and the core idea behind education was to teach and encourage Americans to read the Bible. In order to do that, you had to know how to read.

Today's educational landscape was influenced by many men. One of the largest influencers on education was Horace Mann. He is known by many as the "Father of American Education." His main focus was not only to train teachers, but to influence elementary education for all students. Horace "established the system of separating students by age and grade, which eventually eliminated the multi-grade classroom." (110) This idea spread to the northern states. The southern states did not catch on until the next century. Many would be shocked to know that by the time the southern states caught on to this strategy, approximately thirty-four states had already established laws requiring students to attend school up to a certain age. (111)

As the educational system became more established in America, public schools began implementing segregation by race. However, in 1954, the U.S. Supreme Court ruled in *Brown v. Board of Education* that segregation by race was "inherently unequal" and needed to be abolished. While public schools are no longer able to discriminate against someone based on the color of their skin, there are many theories being taught in American classrooms which are fueling what is known as reverse racism, the most popular being critical race theory.

CRITICAL RACE THEORY

According to the *Encyclopedia Britannica*, critical race theory is defined as "the view that the law and legal institutions are inherently racist and that race itself, instead of being biologically grounded and natural, is a socially constructed concept that is used by white people to further their economic and political interests at the expense of people of color." (112)

Critical race theory is a philosophy that has become a prominent worldview. At its core, it is a form of cultural Marxism. It is a philosophy that categorizes people into two groups--the oppressed and the oppressor. CRT comes cleverly packaged in the name "social justice" and declares that people of color are perpetual victims of "systemic racism." It is educational socialism. At its core, CRT encourages society to blame others for one's shortcomings. Adam blamed Eve. Eve blamed the serpent. Today, people blame others for their own refusal to work hard in order to excel. An educational system infiltrated with CRT restricts the achievers, limiting their potential, and offers unearned opportunities to those less proficient or motivated to excel. Two of the largest problems in our society today are a lack of gratitude for what we have and an unwillingness to take responsibility for our own failures.

The ideas and attitudes of those promoting CRT are diametrically opposed to the American Dream and a biblical worldview. The process is pretty simple. You work hard. You try hard. You put in the effort. You see the results. God honors those that put in the time it takes to succeed. CRT punishes excellence. The reason people are successful is not because of the color of their skin. The reason people fail is not because of the color of their skin. The reason people excel or fail is based on a host of criteria, such as hard work, perseverance, and grit. James Lindsay stated, "Critical race theory conflates white race with western values. Queer theory conflates normalcy with western values. Post-colonial theory conflates being a westerner with western values... Often Marxist feminism conflates being male with western values. Critical Marxism is attacking the western values system." (113) Hard work, individual responsibility, and perseverance lead to prosperity. Marxism leads to the death of a society.

Critical race theory touts the idea that, if you are white, you are a racist born with "white privilege." The idea of "whiteness" is the foundation of critical race theory. Liberals define "whiteness" as a set of normative privileges granted to white-skinned individuals and groups which are "invisible" to those privileged by it. Those who talk about "whiteness" are actually the racist ones.

If you look into most of the recent mass shootings incited by those within the rainbow cult, you'll notice their primary motivation was hate. In the Covenant School Shooting Manifesto (which took way too long to be released), the transgender shooter, Audrey Hale, wanted to kill the white wealthy people. In her manifesto, Aubrey wrote, "Wanna kill all you little cr*ckers, bunch of faggots with your white [privilege], f**k you faggots..." (114) Ironically, she's white and the term "faggot" that she used is a derrogatory slang word used by some (not myself) to describe homosexuals--which she was. This shooter was motivated by the idea that all white people are born racist and with white privilege, but where did this hate stem from? It is sown into the hearts and minds of our youth through our educational system, the media, Hollywood, etc. They are unashamedly indoctrinating children with critical race theory.

Congresswoman Majorie Taylor Green shared a tweet that I agree with: "Every shooter's manifesto should be public. There is absolutely no reason to hide this. Unless, of course, our government wants to hide the fact that these shooters are on SSRIs and usually brainwashed by leftist's propaganda." (115) If a Christian or a normal white person (not a part of the rainbow cult) opened fire on an elementary school killing six innocent people, three of which were children, that manifesto would have been released immediately.

Critical race theory seeks to punish and unfairly scrutinize those who excel, unnecessarily polarizing certain members of society. James Lindsay nailed it when he explained that CRT proponents seek to "scoop up sympathizers to its cause. It is intentionally divisive but intentionally divisive in a particular way so that it will radicalize certain people who it says has a critical race consciousness to its cause." (116)

In 1989, a woman by the name of Peggy McIntosh published an article titled, "White Privilege: Unpacking the Invisible Knapsack." The paper was centered around the notion that white people are born inherently racist. Surprisingly, there was not a single citation for scholarly research or a footnote to be found in her article. Rather, it was based on assumption and opinions. I have absolutely no problem with someone expressing their opinions since this is a First Amendment right. However, I do have a problem when the government imposes assumptions on society that have zero scientific research or data supporting them (especially in the educational system).

In McIntosh's article, she describes her "research" process:

> I decided to try to work on myself at least by identifying some of the daily efforts of white privilege in my life. I have chosen those that I think in my case attach some-what more to skin-color privilege than to class, religion, ethnic status, or geographic location, though of course all these other factors are intricately intertwined. As far as I can tell, my African American coworkers, friends, and acquaintances with whom I come into daily or frequent contact at this particular time... cannot count on most of these conditions... For me, white privilege has turned out to be an elusive and fugitive subject. The pressure to avoid it is great, for in facing it I must give up the myth of meritocracy. If these things are true, this is not such a free country; one's life is not what one makes it; many doors open for certain people through no virtues of their own. These perceptions mean also that my moral condition

is not what I had been led to believe. The appearance of being a good citizen rather than a troublemaker comes in large part from having all sorts of doors open automatically because of my color. (117)

Throughout Peggy's entire article you will hear a continual message of "the oppressed vs. the oppressor."
Where in the world did CRT originate, and when did it begin? When did CRT first start slipping into the educational system? In 1989, Derrick Bell, a professor at Harvard Law School, and others held a conference in Wisconsin where CRT was birthed. Prior to critical race theory, it was the movement of critical legal studies, which, in short, was dedicated to studying how legal institutions serve the more "privileged class" (wealthy) over the "less privileged class" (poor). UCLA School of Public Affairs said, "Critical race theory is an outgrowth of critical legal studies (CLS), which was a leftist movement that challenged traditional legal scholarship." (118)

CRT recognizes that racism is engrained in the fabric and system of American society. The individual racist need not exist to note that institutional racism is pervasive in the dominant culture. This is the analytical lens that CRT uses in examining existing power structures. CRT identifies that these power structures are based on white privilege and white supremacy, which

> perpetuates the marginalization of people of color. CRT also rejects the traditions of liberalism and meritocracy. Legal discourse says that the law is neutral and colorblind, however, CRT challenges this legal "truth" by examining liberalism and meritocracy as a vehicle for self-interest, power, and privilege. (119)

The day after Barack Obama won the 2008 election, Voddie Baucham published a blog post titled, "Barack Obama: A Wolf in Sheep's Clothing." In it he wrote:

> Barack Hussein Obama has been elected the 44th President of the United States of America. The left-wing press is ecstatic, white guilt has been assuaged, Affirmative Action has been vindicated, and socialist Europe loves us again. Now comes the rub… It ain't over! If you think this means that the "America is a racist society" crowd will have to shut up, you've got another thing coming. In fact, watch the press closely in the coming days. There will be a concerted effort to press the opposite point. Jesse Jackson (who said he wanted to castrate Obama a couple of months ago because he had the audacity to call black fathers to account), Al Sharpton, and their ilk will argue that this is merely proof that policies like Affirmative Action work, and such efforts need to be redoubled; not abandoned. They believe we need to continue telling young black boys and girls that they are not smart enough,

and America is not "fair" enough for them to succeed without special help that their white (or asian) counterparts don't need. (120)

This idea of hegemony, which was redefined by an Italian marxist named Antonio Gramsci, is a "complex interlocking of political, social, and cultural forces." (121) Essentially, hegemony is what happens when an elite group imposes their ideologies onto the people through indoctrination and "conditioning" instead of force. This is exactly what they are doing with CRT, among many other issues.

Critical race theory is an extremely harmful ideology that is embedding a victim mentality in the psyche of an entire generation. Make no mistake, the globalist elites have instilled these ideologies through paid propagandists and non-governmental organizations (NGOS) into the educational system to not only indoctrinate the next generation but to create division; divide and conquer.

God Removed

To be frank, I don't believe the problem began when we took prayer and the pledge out of the public school system. I believe the birthdate of our troubles was the day we removed prayer and patriotism from the home. As families have become more relaxed and less deliberate in instilling biblical teachings, prayer practices, and knowledge of American history, the harmful influence of cultural Marxism has started to take root. This shift reflects a broader trend where traditional values and moral education have diminished, allowing ideologies that undermine the foundations of society to gain traction.

When families prioritize less intentional engagement in these critical areas, they risk allowing alternative ideologies to fill the void. This change can lead to a disconnection from historical and spiritual principles that have shaped American culture and identity. It's essential for families to actively engage in teaching and discussing these values to counteract the spread of divisive ideologies. Strengthening the foundation of biblical teachings, prayer, and a thorough understanding of American history can help preserve the integrity of family and society against the influences of cultural Marxism.

It metastasized into the courts in 1958. The legal removal of prayer in schools was achieved in the 1962 Supreme Court case: *Engel v. Vitale*. This case began in 1958 when a man by the name of Steven Engel collaborated with other parents to sue the state of New York over prayer being offered in public schools. They argued that mandating the students' participation in the prayer was "unconstitutional" and violated the principle of "separation of Church and State." Michael Brown, a Christian apologist quoted, "A plain-text reading of the Amendment says 'no law… no law shall be made to impede free exercise of religion.' So they say 'separation of Church and

State.' I say there would be no State without the Church." (122) In 1962, the final ruling of this case declared that the state of New York violated the First Amendment's establishment clause. Justice Potter Stewart stated that "he failed to understand how children choosing to recite a prayer established a religion…" He added that requiring them not to do so went further toward violating the establishment clause than letting them choose." (123) The removal of God went even further by banning mandatory Bible readings in public schools in 1963 with the Supreme Court case *Murray v. Curlett.* (124) Instead of teaching children that there is a Creator who knows the exact number of hairs on their head, the school system is teaching students that we evolved from apes. If we came from nothing and we are ending with nothing; we are, therefore, just walking zombies with no purpose or intended design.

Throughout history, dictators and communist leaders characteristically first removed religion, prayer, and the faith of its people in order to break down the society. The removal of God and prayer from public education is another step closer to the global elites' 2030 Agenda.

Sex Ed Leading to Gender Ed

One of the most pervasive ideologies being taught in the education system is gender ideology. Schools across America stock sexually explicit books in the libraries with instructions on how to masturbate and how to perform particular sex acts. LGBTQ flags are posted in classrooms, teachers encourage the usage of pronouns, and school counselors advise students not to tell their parents about their feelings. The list goes on and on. Many schools have also adopted policies to be gender "inclusive," specifically in regards to bathrooms. In the previous chapter, I gave an example of the horrific result of adopting policies that allow male students (who think they are girls) to enter the women's locker rooms and bathrooms.

The question is: How did gender ideology seep into our educational system? From the extensive research I have done, I can trace it all back to when we introduced sex education into the classroom. As shocking as it may seem, there actually used to be programs in public schools encouraging abstinence until marriage. In 1981, Congress passed the Adolescent Family Life Act (AFLA), which funded educational programs to promote abstinence and self-discipline until marriage. This received much of its initial support from the Republican Party. Shortly after this passed, the American Civil Liberties Union (ACLU) pushed back heavily against it, claiming it was a violation of "separation of Church and State," specifically because of its opposition to abortion. (125) However, the goals in abstinence-only programs include: (126)

A. Has as its exclusive purpose, teaching the social, psychological, and health gains to be realized by abstaining from sexual activity;

B. Teaches abstinence from sexual activity outside marriage as the expected standard for all school-age children;

C. Teaches that abstinence from sexual activity is the only certain way to avoid out-of-wedlock pregnancy, sexually transmitted diseases, and other associated health problems;

E. Teaches that a mutually faithful, monogamous marriage is the expected standard of sexual activity;
Teaches that sexual activity outside the context of marriage is likely to have harmful psychological and physical effects;

F. Teaches that bearing children out-of-wedlock is likely to have harmful consequences for the child, the child's parents, and society;

G. Teaches young people how to reject sexual advances and how alcohol and drug use increases vulnerability to sexual advances; and

H. Teaches the importance of attaining self-sufficiency before engaging in sexual activity.

Although federal funding is still available for abstinence-only education, very few schools actually implement it into their sex ed. Instead, they primarily use what is called comprehensive sex education.

It comes as no surprise that the majority of the comprehensive sex ed curriculum was shaped by the feminist movement and largely funded and provided by Planned Parenthood. (127) In 1964, a doctor by the name of Mary Calderone, who was the medical director for Planned Parenthood's Federation of America, founded the Sexuality Information and Educational Council of the United States (SIECUS). (128) To be frank, SIECUS took the fledgling ideas that Alfred Kinsey proposed about sex (mentioned briefly in the previous chapter) and made them a reality. During the 1980s, copious debates ensued regarding the extent of sex ed in public schools. In 1990, SIECUS held the National Guidelines Task Force, a panel of experts to design curriculum for sex education. Just one year later, the Guidelines for Comprehensive Sexual Education for K-12 were released. This included information on human sexuality, reproduction, pregnancy, sexual orientation, gender identity, masturbation, abortion, sexual abuse, sexually transmitted infections, among a host of other topics. Gender ideology slowly slithered its way into public schools nearly thirty years ago under the guise of "sex education."

In 2024, we have teachers telling students about queer sex, giving them dildos, butt plugs, and different sex toys. (129) Nearly every public school in America has pornographic books in the library that depict oral sex, sexual intercourse, masturbation, rape, and incest. Additionally, several bills and pieces of legislation have been drafted (some even passed in blue states) that remove parents' rights and enable children to act autonomously and make their own medical decisions. In July of 2022, the office for Civil Rights within the Department of Education (which I believe should be abolished) released a proposal for new rules under Title IX of the Education Amendments of 1972: "If passed, the rules would, among other things, ramp up the pressure on school districts to adopt policies that will facilitate students' gender transitions, even without the knowledge or consent of their parents." (130) Essentially, the Biden administration is creating a school-to-clinic pipeline. It is absolutely despicable that this is being debated. No school should ever facilitate medical decisions for students.

The feminist movement, along with Planned Parenthood, replaced morality with immorality in our public school system. One does not need to be a Christian in order to encourage abstinence and behaviors that have been proven to protect the health of children and adolescents. If you want to prevent unplanned pregnancies and sexually transmitted diseases, encourage abstinence until marriage. It's that simple.

Let me be clear that I do believe schools should teach biology and human anatomy, but what many people don't realize is that the Bible teaches that the act of sex is spiritual. For example, the scriptures explain in 1 Corinthians 6:16, "Or do you not know that he who is joined to a prostitute becomes one body with her? For, as it is written, 'The two will become one flesh.'" The government has no business teaching children about sex. Education about sexuality should be addressed by families and the local church.

The founder of Fight the New Drug, Clay Olson, stated in reference to sex ed, "This material is more aggressive, more harmful, more violent, more degrading and damaging than any other time in the history of the world. And this generation growing up is dealing with it at an intensity and scale no other generation in the history of the world has ever had to." (131) This should be the parents' job, as it has been until fifty to eighty years ago.

Parental Authority

Part and parcel of removing God entirely from the education system and in society in general is removing parental authority. Thomas Jefferson said, "If it is believed that these elementary schools will be better managed by the government and council or any general authority of the government, than by the parents within each ward, it is belief against all experience." (132)

Up until really the 2000s, Americans have by and large stood firm on the belief that parents can arbitrate what is or is not best for their children. In *Parham v. J.R.,* Chief Justice Warren Burger stated in 1979 that the law "has recognized that natural bonds of affection lead parents to act in the best interests of their children." (133) Unfortunately, the judges that Barack Obama appointed while he was in office are making it increasingly more challenging for parents to steward their children without interference from the state.

The feminist movement produced the idea that both parents should be out of the home working. But why was the government (alongside the feminist movement) pushing that both parents should be out of the home? Well, when both parents are out of the home, the children will be placed in public school, and the government can shape their minds. This is, in fact, a communist and Marxist idea.

Right now, many public educators are telling our children that they don't really need their parents. The Biden administration's White House Press Secretary stated, "These are our kids. They belong to all of us." (134) Many of you may remember when Hillary Clinton said that it takes a village to raise a child and children in general. What most didn't realize about her statement was that she was insinuating that the United States government should be the "parent" over our children. They (the globalist elites) believe your children belong to the state—the government. The feminist movement created a smart plan to accomplish their mission—move Mom out of the house so the government can move in. It has always been about the government becoming the parent. This is literally Mao, China.

California, the state run by the Communist Chinese Party, recently introduced a statewide system they call "Cradle-to-Career." The website states: "The California Cradle-to-Career Data System connects individuals and organizations with trusted information and resources, providing insights into critical milestones in the pipeline from early care to K–12 to higher education, skills training, and employment. The data system empowers individuals to reach their full potential and fosters evidence-based decision-making to help California build a more equitable future." (135) The same thing happens in Communist China, where they pick what the children do, what they will study, and who they will become.

Barack Obama and his cartoon film, "The Life of Julia," demonstrated how the welfare programs of the Obama Administration would sustain Americans. Essentially, this short slideshow depicted how Obama's policies would help one woman over the course of her entire lifetime (cradle-to-grave). An article published by CNN in 2012 stated something you don't want to overlook:

Last week, President Obama's campaign launched a fictional storybook ad called, "The Life of Julia." The slide show narrative follows Julia, a cartoon character, from age 3 to age 67 and explains how Obama's policies, from Head Start to Obamacare to mandated contraception coverage to Medicare reform, would provide Julia with a better life than Mitt Romney or Paul Ryan could. For Republicans, Julia's story might seem like a joke too good to be true, but they should take it very seriously. Because buried within "The Life of Julia" is the ideological vision of modern liberalism--to create a state that takes care of its people from cradle to grave. The story of Julia is a microcosm of Obama's vision for America and emblematic of his view of the government's role in an individual's life. (136)

In the same article, CNN went on to report:

"The Life of Julia" has done what many conservatives have failed to do so far--outline in exacting detail what modern Democratic policy wants for individuals. Here we have Obama's 21st century synthesis of the Great Society, New Deal and New Frontier. Julia's entire life is defined by her interactions with the state. Government is everywhere and each step of her life is tied to a government program. Notably absent in her story is any relationship with a husband, family, church or community, except a "community" garden

Education

where she works post-retirement. Instead, the state has taken their place and is her primary relationship. (137)

Throughout Julia's entire life, the government is there to "help." This reminds me of Ronald Reagan's famous quip from 1986: "The nine most terrifying words in the English language are: 'I'm from the government, and I'm here to help.'" (138) But the film, "The Life of Julia," reveals the left's goal to remove private property completely, which includes parental rights over your children. This is one of the ways the Marxist elites have infiltrated the family. Over time, they persuade naive parents to relinquish the family steering wheel and place the government in the driver's seat. When Mao came to power in China, one of his first acts was to remove parental rights. Every single house was required to display a picture of Mao so no one would forget that he was "their god."

I love George Washington's quote: "All I am I owe to my own mother. I attribute all my success in life to the moral, intellectual, and physical education I received from my mother." (139) As I write this book, I can wholeheartedly give full credit to my parents for instilling godly principles and values into my heart. As I will discuss more in detail later, I believe the greatest problem in our country is the breakdown of the family. Parents are more disconnected from their children's hearts than ever before. The lack of relationship between the child and parent is evident in today's society. Out of the many core principles that my parents have instilled in my siblings and me, the idea that we must ultimately make decisions for ourselves (self-govern) has been immensely important. Parents can teach their children these principles all day long, but children have to make the conscious decision to live a life of holiness, to speak the truth, to work hard, etc.

> "I call heaven and earth to record this day against you, that I have set before you life and death, blessing and cursing: therefore, choose life, that both thou and thy seed may live: that thou mayest love the LORD thy God, and that thou mayest obey his voice, and that thou mayest cleave unto him: for he is thy life, and the length of thy days: that thou mayest dwell in the land which the LORD sware unto thy fathers, to Abraham, to Isaac, and to Jacob, to give them."
> (Deuteronomy 30:19-20, KJV)

God offered two choices, and He relegated the responsibility to make the choice and reap the consequences for each individual. In our society as a whole, nobody wants to take responsibility. Look at student loan debt. Students want taxpayers to pay for the debt they incurred because they do not want to take responsibility. How about credit card debt? Why should you receive a bailout when you frivolously spent the money? What about abortion? Why should an innocent baby be murdered and given no chance of life because of your choices?

Education

Other important concepts that my parents have instilled into my siblings and me are intrinsic motivation and being able to think for ourselves. Hard work, perseverance, and a drive to succeed at life are important characteristics all parents should seek to produce in their children. Instead of sitting in front of a television together, wouldn't it be more beneficial to sit at the dining room table at dinnertime and discuss why a biblical worldview matters? If parents do not teach and train their children through repeated productive conversations, who will? How will they know how to apply the Bible in the real world?

> "And ye shall teach them to your children,
> speaking of them when thou sittest in thine house,
> and when thou walkest by the way, when
> thou liest down, and when thou risest up."
> (Deuteronomy 11:19, KJV)

Again, parents can teach their children all this information, but if it is not practically applied, it is worthless. Many people ask how to get my generation engaged and active, and, sadly, I'm asking and wondering the same thing! I truly cannot get my generation (Gen Z) engaged until I get the parents involved. The powerful impact upon children by two parents participating in civic matters cannot be understated!

Higher Education

Penny Nance, the CEO of Concerned Women for America and a woman whom I highly esteem, took her son to a freshman orientation at the University at Virginia Tech in 2019. As students arrived, they were handed a name badge that included their "preferred pronouns," which was required to add when registering. In an article with The Federalist, Penny shared the experience in greater detail: "The college filled the next two hours with speaker after speaker who introduced themselves with not just their names and titles but also preferred pronouns—as in, 'Hi, my name is Penny Nance, and I identify as she and her.' At first, parents were slightly surprised; by the end, they were mad." Later in the article, Penny wrote:

> Why should a public university force a young man or woman struggling with identity issues, for example, to disclose those personal details and prominently display them on a name badge? Gender dysphoria is real, and the small number of students struggling deserve to be treated with dignity and kindness. Why should a public institution be allowed to violate teachers' First Amendment rights by bullying them into using the made-up terms they/them, zie/zim, ey/em (or about 60 more) instead of she/her or he/him? The reordering of centuries of grammar usage is an offensive overcorrection, and it bullies Christians, Muslims, and other

Education

students into violating their consciences to appease a small group of nonsensical identity politics warriors. (140)

This is the reality at almost every single college campus in America.

The first school of higher education in the United States to survive was started in 1636. This school was called Harvard College. The college centered its education around a particular verse in the Bible—John 17:3. When the school was first chartered they declared:

> Let every student be plainly instructed and earnestly pressed to consider well the main end of his life and studies is to know God and Jesus Christ which is eternal life (John 17:3), and therefore to lay Christ in the bottom as the only foundation of all sound knowledge and learning. And seeing the Lord only giveth wisdom, let everyone seriously set himself by prayer in secret to seek it out of Him (Proverbs 2:3). Everyone shall exercise himself in reading the Scripture twice a day that he shall be ready to give such an account of his proficiency therein. (141)

Harvard College was dedicated to the mission of raising students to be warriors and teachers of the Word of God. In the Harvard Graduate's Magazine, it lists the two mottos that Harvard College stood by: "For the Glory of

Christ" and "For Christ and the Church."

Fast-forward to the year 2002. *Harvard Magazine* published an article titled, "Abolish the White Race." Shamelessly, the author threatened, "Make no mistake about it: we intend to keep bashing the dead white males, and the live ones, and the females too, until the social construct known as 'the white race' is destroyed—not 'deconstructed' but destroyed." (142)

The point stands that nearly all the way up until the late 1800s, the goal of higher education was to teach and instruct students teachings from the Bible and absolute truth, as well as how to be equipped in order to teach others. It was recorded by James Angell that nearly 90% of state universities continued with chapel services, one-fourth required chapel attendance, and a quarter required regular church attendance in addition to the chapel service.

Taking Action & Protecting Next Gen

Public education's agenda includes teaching children what to think and not how to think.

H.L. Mencken said:

> The most erroneous assumption is to the effect that the aim of public education is to fill the young of the species with knowledge and awaken their intelligence, and so make them fit to discharge the duties of citizenship

in an enlightened and independent manner. Nothing could be further from the truth. The aim of public education is not to spread enlightenment at all; it is simply to reduce as many individuals as possible to the same safe level, to breed and train a standardized citizenry, to put down dissent and originality. That is its aim in the United States, whatever the pretensions of politicians, pedagogues and other such mountebanks, and that is its aim everywhere else. (143)

Parents, stop sending your children to the Lion's Den. Stop sending them to state-sponsored schools whose main goal is to indoctrinate your children with "woke" propaganda and tear at the allegiance toward you and God Almighty. Stop believing the lie that sending your children to public school is a way for them to be a light in the darkness, because more times than not, your children are the ones being impacted and influenced. Buck the system!

It is time that we completely eliminate and abolish the Department of Education. There is no fixing it.

*** **TAKE A** *CHANCE!* ***

Starting with Samuel Adams and Thomas Jefferson's emphasis on a well-educated public for a strong nation, discover how American schooling initially included biblical principles and moral lessons. Examine how CRT challenges individual achievement and divides society into oppressors and victims. Especially, consider the long-term consequences of abandoning meritocracy and discuss CRT's impacts with your peers. You can engage in activities that include creating presentations on historical shifts in education, researching and debating CRT, and discussing ways to promote values like perseverance and responsibility.

"Whoever sheds man's blood,
by man his blood shall be shed; For in the
image of God He made man."

—Genesis 9:6

Chapter 7
Abortion

The idea of "overpopulation" and the use of birth control and contraceptives can be traced back to the framework of Malthusianism. Reverend Thomas Malthus published *An Essay On The Principle of Population* anonymously in 1798. Much of his book was dedicated to what is known as Malthus' Iron Law of Population. Later, in 1877, the Malthusian League was founded in London, England with the mission of promoting contraception to "limit family size." (144) Essentially, in Malthusianism, the solution to the "overpopulation problem" is contraception, which limits the number of children per family. "The neo-Malthusian position found favor with the elite sentiments on the issue of overpopulation. The elite, threatened by the growing numbers of commoners, considered birth control as an important means of checking future conflict over their property." (145)

The eugenics movement was largely influenced by the Malthusian theory of reducing the population. The difference between the eugenics movement and the Malthusian theory is that eugenics reduces the population

133

down to just "valuable" members of society, whereas the Malthusian theory asserts that our planet can only sustain a certain amount of people. Francis Galton, author of *Human Faculty,* coined the term "eugenics," defining it as "the science which deals with all influences that improve the inborn qualities of a race; also with those that develop them to the utmost advantage." (146) Galton reiterated his idea to "bring as many influences as can be reasonably employed, to cause the useful classes in the community to contribute more than their proportion to the next generation." (147)

In 1914, Margaret Sanger coined the term "birth control," and, in 1916, the first Planned Parenthood clinic dedicated to providing women with information on birth control opened in Brooklyn, New York. In 1917, Sanger launched *The Birth Control Review,* where it frequently reiterated the goal of its parent organization, The American Birth Control League. Their creed? "To promote eugenic birth selection throughout the United States so that there may be more well-born and fewer ill-born children—a stronger, healthier, and more intelligent society." (148)

By 1920, she had initiated an entire birth control movement. Sanger believed that birth control and other contraceptives were the prerequisite for women to experience true freedom. She argued, "No woman can call herself free who does not own and control her own body." (149) However, Sanger was simultaneously promoting birth control as a medical issue to enhance the eugenics aspect.

Margaret Sanger grew up in a family of eleven children, and her mother's health was declining due to problematic pregnancies and miscarriages. At age fifty, she died of tuberculosis. Her mother's experiences and untimely death heavily influenced her advocacy for birth control, and later, abortion. According to Planned Parenthood, "In 1923, Sanger opened the Birth Control Clinical Research Bureau in Manhattan. That same year, Sanger incorporated the American Birth Control League, an ambitious new organization that examined the global impact of population control, disarmament, and famine. The two organizations eventually merged in 1942 to become Planned Parenthood Federation of America, Inc. (PFFA)." (150)

I believe it is also important to accentuate Sanger's roots in eugenics, which propelled her into birth control and family planning advocacy. Sanger stated, "Before eugenists and others who are laboring for racial betterment can succeed, they must first clear the way for Birth Control. Like the advocates of Birth Control, the eugenists, for instance, are seeking to assist the race toward the elimination of the unfit... Birth control of itself, by freeing the reproductive instinct from its present chains, will make a better race... Eugenics without birth control seems to us a house built upon the sands. It is at the mercy of the rising stream of the unfit." (151) The woman behind the nation's top provider of sex education, abortion, contraception, etc., was a racist white woman who identified herself as a eugenist in nearly all of her writings. Sanger even spoke to the women's auxiliary of the Ku Klux Klan (KKK) in 1926 to promote contraception and birth control. She also endorsed the Supreme Court's decision in *Buck v. Bell*, which ruled that states who see members of society as "unfit" can forcibly sterilize them.

In 1924, pushing more of the "overpopulation" propaganda, Raymond B. Fosdick, president of the Rockefeller Foundation, wrote a letter to J.D. Rockefeller Jr. He wrote:

> Personally I believe that the problem of population constitutes one of the great perils of the future and if something is not done along the lines that these people are suggesting, we shall hand down to our children a world in which scramble for food and the means of subsistence will be far more bitter than anything we know at the present. Scientists are pointing hopefully to such methods as Mrs. Sanger and her associates are advocating, and these two organizations are doing their best to disseminate knowledge of contraceptive practices, as far as the present somewhat archaic law allows them to. (152)

Rockefeller allegedly gave an anonymous donation to Sanger as a result of that letter.

During the early 1930s, the Rockefeller Foundation circulated a memorandum which declared: "Birth Control has the support of many of the best and most intelligent people in the world, and it also has the support of some persons whose mental balance is not the best. In between these two classes, we find the people who hold debatable opinions, the most capable group being the eugenicists." (153)

Some of the greatest momentum in the advancement of the birth control movement--not just in America, but globally--was when Sanger founded the International Planned Parenthood Federation (IPPF) in 1954. This organization (and much of the birth control, abortion, and feminist movement) was funded by the Rockefellers. Margaret Sanger, the Rockefellers, and other nefarious elites didn't merely target America with their despicable eugenics ideology; this was a global enterprise. The Rockefeller Brothers Fund donated approximately $150,000 (the equivalent of about $1,750,000 today) to Sanger's Planned Parenthood Federation to support her efforts as she traveled across America and into other countries sharing her ideas on family planning and birth control. "(154) According to the Rockefeller Brothers Fund, they later contributed to Planned Parenthood to launch programs for childcare, prenatal medical care, abortions, public education, and projects in African American communities.

Let's do a quick recap. Margaret Sanger, a racist white woman, founded Planned Parenthood with the mission of providing birth control information and advice to women. Sanger saw abortion and birth control as the answer to economic disparity and the road to freedom for women. She also wanted to exterminate the "unfit," which included Africans. I would suggest that if eugenics and population control were the end goals for Sanger, then birth control was the means by which they would be achieved. I would argue that Sanger's disturbing mission goes even deeper than "controlling the population." This is about separating everyone into two classes: the elites versus the peasants or, in modern vernacular, the oppressors versus the oppressed.

Before going further, I want to mention the harms of teenage girls or women in general being put on birth control pills. It has been treated as candy by Big Pharma and is prescribed to young girls for nearly any issue regarding their menstrual cycle, preventing pregnancy as a whole, hormones, etc. Statistics have shown that teenage girls who take birth control are 130% more likely to experience clinical depression. (155)

Within the last couple of years, Planned Parenthood separated themselves from their founder, stating, "Margaret Sanger's racism and belief in eugenics are in direct opposition to Planned Parenthood's mission. Planned Parenthood denounces Margaret Sanger's belief in eugenics. Further, Planned Parenthood denounces the history and legacy of anti-Blackness in anti-gynecology and the reproductive rights movement, and the mistreatment that continues against Black, Indigenous, and other people of color in this country." (156)

It is quite interesting to note how the left constantly changes their narrative. Their representation of Margaret Sanger has moved from "population control leader and promoter of eugenics" to "advocate for reproductive health." Look at climate change. At one point, the world was going to freeze up, then it was going to burn up, and now we just have a climate crisis. The verbiage is constantly changed to create confusion. The goal remains the same, but the deceptive language and means of attaining that goal are cunningly crafted.

Betty Friedman, who will be discussed in greater detail in the next chapter, was a well-known radical feminist. She founded one of the most widely known feminist organizations: National Organization for Women founded in 1966 (NOW). According to their website, "NOW's purpose is to take action through intersectional grassroots activism to promote feminist ideals, lead societal change, eliminate discrimination, and achieve and protect the equal rights of all women and girls in all aspects of social, political, and economic life." (157) NOW also has six core issues, the first being Reproductive Rights and Justice. Economic Justice, Racial Justice, Ending Violence Against Women, LGBTQIA+ Rights, and Constitutional Equality constitute the other five objectives. (158) Friedman played a large role in advocating for "reproductive health" and the feminist movement as a whole, co-founding the National Association for the

Repeal of Abortion Laws (NARAL) with Dr. Bernard N. Nathanson.

In February 1969, Friedman made the connection between the second wave feminist movement and the movement to legalize access to abortion in a speech at the First National Conference on Abortion Laws in Chicago, Illinois, where she declared that women's rights included the ability to control their reproduction. She also mentioned the hazards of illicit abortions and described situations in which women endangered their lives by receiving abortions from unlicensed doctors. She argued that legalizing abortion could help prevent those situations. Friedan modified the Women's Bill of Rights endorsed by NOW to include the right to have an abortion outside of the extenuating circumstances of rape and life endangerment. During all of these efforts, Friedan and her husband divorced in 1969. Friedan continued to advocate for the benefits of the repeal of anti-abortion legislation, which helped set a national stage for the U.S. Supreme Court decision of *Roe v. Wade* in 1973. The ruling of the case affirmed women's right to have abortions up through the second trimester of pregnancy without any state regulation. (159)

LEGISLATION TO ROE

In 1965, the U.S. Supreme Court ruled in the landmark case, *Griswold v. Connecticut*, that states could no longer deny the sale of any contraception to couples that are married. Title X of the Public Health Services Act became law in 1970. This established "government funding" (which really just means taxpayer-funded) for family planning and sex education programs. Nearly seven years later, in 1972, the United States Supreme Court struck down the law (Eisenstadt v. Baird) that banned anyone from distributing any type of contraceptive to unmarried individuals. Regardless of relationship status, anyone was permitted to access birth control from their doctor. During the early '70s, states were beginning to legalize abortions in particular cases. New York was one of the first states to legalize abortion, and the first Planned Parenthood to offer abortion procedures was in Syracuse, NY. (160)

Just three years later, in the landmark case, *Roe v. Wade*, the United States Supreme Court ruled in favor of abortion within the first three months in all fifty states. This case changed the trajectory of our nation for almost fifty years.

Many things have happened for the multi-*billion* dollar abortion industry since 1973. In October of the year 2000, the FDA approved mifepristone (RU-486), which is more commonly known as the abortion pill. In 2005, Planned Parenthood began administering hormone replacement therapy. By 2013, Plan B was not just available over the counter for women eighteen or older, but for all ages. However, when George W. Bush became president, he reinstated the gag rule originally introduced by the Reagan administration. Bush stated, "It is my conviction that taxpayer funds should not be used to pay for abortions or advocate or actively promote abortion, either here or abroad." (161) Chronicling their history, Planned Parenthood's website remarked about this supposed setback: "Funding for 'abstinence-only' programs increased, leaving students across the country without medically accurate sexual health information." (162) It is no surprise that they are mocking abstinence-only programs. A few years later, in 2009, President Barack Obama overturned the gag rule, smugly proclaiming that his administration cared and was committed to protecting women's reproductive health.

ABORTION METHODS

I believe it's imperative to understand what the abortion process entails. For each trimester, there are different abortion methods. The most common abortion method in the first trimester is the abortion pill. This is considered a "medical abortion," but I would submit that there is absolutely nothing medical about the abortion pill. Medical is defined in two ways: (1) relating to or concerned with physicians or the practice of medicine; (2) requiring or devoted to medical treatment. (163) According to the World Health Organization (WHO), "The use of medical methods of abortion requires the back-up of vacuum aspiration, either on-site or through referral to another health-care facility in case of failed or incomplete abortion." (164) This was a statement written in an article titled "Safe Abortions."

There is absolutely nothing safe about murdering the life of a growing and living human. The abortion pill itself, mifepristone (RU-486), essentially blocks the production of progesterone and cuts off blood and nutrients for the baby. Within a day or two, the mother will take another pill, misoprostol, which causes the mother to have contractions and bleed, forcing the baby out. (165) Another abortion method (employed usually up to fourteen weeks) is called a dilation and curettage abortion (D&C abortion): "An abortionist uses metal rods or medication to dilate the woman's cervix and gain access to the uterus, where the baby resides. The abortionist then inserts a suction catheter to vacuum the child from the womb. The suction machine has a force approximately 10 to 20 times the force of a household vacuum cleaner. The procedure is completed as the abortionist uses a sharp metal device called a curette to empty the remains of the child from the mother's uterus." (166)

The abortion procedure in the second trimester is called a D&E (Dilation and Evacuation). According to a former abortionist, "A dilation (dilatation) and evacuation abortion, D&E, is a surgical abortion procedure during which an abortionist first dilates the woman's cervix and then uses instruments to dismember and extract the baby from the uterus. The D&E abortion procedure is usually performed between thirteen and twenty-four weeks LMP (that is thirteen to twenty-four weeks after the first day of the woman's last menstrual period)." (167) A D&E abortion typically takes around two to three days in order to prepare the cervix. Live Action has done an Abortion Procedure Project which has been approved by physicians (regarding its accuracy), and one of the videos detailing a D&E abortion states, "The most difficult part of the procedure is usually finding, grasping, and crushing the baby's head." (168) During second trimester abortions, the dilation increases the chance of cervical damage, and, unfortunately, this can prohibit the woman from being able to carry further pregnancies to term. According to The National Library of Medicine, "During 1988–1997, the overall death rate for women obtaining legally induced abortions was 0.7 per 100,000 legal induced abortions. The risk of death increased exponentially by 38% for each additional week of gestation." (169)

During third trimester abortions (25+ weeks), abortionists perform what is called an induction abortion. This type of abortion procedure usually takes around three to four days. The risks only increase with this type of abortion, and most physicians consider this to be the most traumatizing abortion as it essentially mimics birth. On the first day of the procedure, the abortionist injects a lethal dose of digoxin or potassium chloride into the baby's heart to stop the heartbeat. The injection causes the baby to go into cardiac arrest. This is nothing less than intentional murder. If the abortionist misses the heart, the chemical will still terminate the baby; however, the rate of death is excruciatingly slow. After the abortionist administers the injection, the woman will be given misoprostol to widen the cervix and begin dilation, and another medication, pitocin, is typically given over the course of the first day to cause contractions to begin. On the second day, to confirm that the baby is dead, they will complete an ultrasound. If the baby is still alive, oftentimes they will inject a second dose. On day three or four (it is case-by-case), the woman delivers the dead baby. "If the child does not come out whole, the procedure becomes a D&E, or a dilation and evacuation. The abortionist uses clamps and forceps to dismember and remove the baby piece by piece." (170)

The Reality

If you are paying attention to our culture, you will notice that liberals do not want to see abortion procedure videos because they reveal the truth about this barbaric, gruesome practice. They refuse to watch what they justify. To them, ignorance is bliss. They will argue with you and name-call, but they won't scientifically explain how it is physically and psychologically beneficial for women to have abortions. Further, progressives and feminists cannot explain why it is morally justifiable. The truth?

Murdering the unborn is morally repugnant, physically detrimental, and psychologically oppressive. It spits in the eye of a life-giving God who commanded us not to murder but to respect life from inception to its end. They have no case. Truly, pro-choice adherents don't believe a fertilized egg is a baby because they don't value the Author of Life. They are in defiance of a God who deserves their love and obedience. They shake their fists and rebel against Genesis 1:28, Psalm 139:13-18, and Jeremiah 1:5.

> "Then God blessed them,
> and God said to them, 'Be fruitful and multiply;
> fill the earth and subdue it…'"
> (Genesis 1:28, NKJV)

"For You formed my inward parts; You covered me in my mother's womb. I will praise You, for I am fearfully and wonderfully made; Marvelous are Your works, And that my soul knows very well. My frame was not hidden from You, When I was made in secret, And skillfully wrought in the lowest parts of the earth. Your eyes saw my substance, being yet unformed. And in Your book they all were written, The days fashioned for me, When as yet there were none of them." (Psalm 139:13-16, NKJV)

> "Before I formed you in the womb I knew you,
> before you were born I set you apart; I appointed
> you as a prophet to the nations."
> (Jeremiah 1:5, NIV)

> "But indeed, O man, who are you to reply against God? Will the thing formed say to him who formed it, 'Why have you made me like this?'"
> (Romans 9:20, NKJV)

People who have made themselves gods do not value life, creating their own standards and rules for living; therefore, it is easy for them to claim it's not a baby. The arrogance is staggering yet understandable when you understand that people whose God is not the Lord serve a different master. The Bible teaches that you are either a child of God or a child of the devil. You are either walking in the light, or you're walking in darkness.

Where and when does a criminal commit crime? In the dark. Planned Parenthood is spiritual darkness. Even though the lights are physically on in the building, the people that work there are groping in the dark as servants of Satan. Their father is the devil (as Jesus taught), and it is their nature to defy God and hate the light.

The left does not want to see abortion videos because they do not want to be confronted with the truth and be pricked in their consciences. They do not want to face the reality that, whether it's the first, second, or third trimester, there really is a living and moving baby inside the mother's womb--a baby who feels pain and deserves protection. The gory and inhumane process is indefensible. How can it possibly be okay to murder a baby you feel moving inside of you?

Impact on Women, Men, and Families

The abortion industry is a multi-billion dollar industry, and they stay in business because Christians have bowed to the altar of influence over speaking the truth. We have labeled the issue of life (just as every other issue mentioned in this book) as political. I believe that pastors and Christians who refuse to speak out against abortion and the importance of protecting life have blood on their hands. Because the church has refused to speak out against abortion, we have created a hollow society that does not esteem life.

Abortion is not just the holocaust of the unborn; it devastates the very soul of society. It is emotionally, physically, and spiritually ruinous to both the mother and father. The impact it has upon humanity cannot be overstated. Planned Parenthood and abortion clinics might explain that women "...may have a range of emotions after having an abortion. Most people feel relief, but sometimes people feel sad or regretful. This is totally normal." (171) By suppressing the slew of statistics and risks that come from abortion, providers are the blind leading the blind, and everyone's falling unsuspectingly into the ditch. There have been several studies conducted showing the impact abortion has on the mother alone. One, in particular, was conducted by the *British Journal of Psychiatry* in 2011. In this study, researchers were able to find drastic mental health changes and declines in women who have had abortions. In the study, they examined the medical information of 877,000 women, and 164,000 of them had undergone an abortion in their past. "Women who had undergone an abortion experienced an 81% increased risk of mental health problems, and nearly 10% of the incidence of mental health problems was shown to be attributable to abortion. The strongest subgroup estimates of increased risk occurred when abortion was compared with term pregnancy and when the outcomes pertained to substance use and suicidal behaviour." (172) The term "health problems" broadly describes that women who have abortions are 34% more likely to develop an anxiety disorder, 37% more likely to experience depression, 110% more likely to abuse alcohol, 155% more likely to commit suicide, and 220% more likely to abuse marijuana. (173)

Many often forget the impact that abortion has on men and fathers. The co-founder of Rachel's Vineyard and a leader of the Father Forever initiative of Silent No More, Kevin Burke, remarked, "Men do not always recognize the symptoms they experience as having their roots in an abortion decision––but scratch the surface and you will see it… They may struggle to make commitments, to be emotionally present to their current wives and children, to embrace their role as spiritual and moral leader in the home… deep down they aborted their son or daughter in the past." (174)

In her article, "A Study of Suffering After Abortion,"

Jean Boydell writes about a psychiatrist, Dr. Julius Fogel, who also happened to be an abortionist. Dr. Fogel was interviewed by the *Wanderer Magazine* published back in April of 1989. In the interview, he discussed the psychological trauma abortion had caused in his own patients dating back to the '80s. Dr. Fogel stated:

> I've had patients who had an abortion a year or two ago... women who did the best thing at the time for themselves... but it still bothers them. Many come in... some are just mute, some hostile. Some burst out crying... there is no question in my mind that we are disturbing a life process. The trauma may sink into the unconscious and never surface in the woman's lifetime... but a psychological price is paid. It may be alienation, it may be pushing away from human warmth, perhaps a hardening of the maternal instinct. Something happens on the deeper levels of a woman's consciousness when she destroys a pregnancy. I know this as a psychiatrist. (175)

STAGES OF PREGNANCY AND FETAL DEVELOPMENT

First Trimester

As the fertilized egg grows, a water-tight sac forms around it. This is called an amniotic sac, and it helps cushion the growing embryo. During this time period, the placenta will also develop. Facial features of the embryo begin to emerge around week five. Between weeks five and eight, the digestive tract and sensory organs begin to develop. The heart starts to mature and beat around four to five weeks but cannot normally be detected until six to seven weeks.

By the end of the first trimester, the fetus is fully formed. All the organs and limbs are present but will continue to grow. Around week twelve, the baby is around four inches long and typically nearing one ounce.

Second Trimester

The second trimester is sometimes considered the best part of pregnancy. Usually morning sickness has subsided and any severe discomfort has faded. During this period, the baby's facial features really begin to emerge. The fingers, toes, eyelids, eyelashes, nails, and hair are formed. In addition, around twenty weeks of gestation, the genitalia appears, allowing physicians to detect the gender (male or female since there are only two options). The skin is covered with a whitish coating called vernix caseosa. Every aspect of pregnancy reveals how awesome our God is, but I find it absolutely incredible that God tenderly provided a substance (the vernix caseosa) to protect fetal skin from long exposure of amniotic fluid. By the end of the sixth month, the baby is twelve inches long and around two pounds. In weeks twenty-five through twenty-eight, hearing is fully developed and the amniotic fluid begins to diminish.

Third Trimester

This is the final stretch of pregnancy. Between weeks twenty-nine and thirty-two, the brain is rapidly developing, and the baby can hear and see. The lungs are still frail at this time, though. The fetus will continue to fill out during weeks thirty-three through thirty-six, and the lungs will be nearing full development at this stage. The baby has full reflexes, can blink, close the eyes, turn the head, grasp firmly, and respond to light and touch well.

The Truth

Abortion is modern-day slavery. I would even suggest that abortion and slavery are two different sins against humanity, driven by the same evil, dehumanizing spirit. I believe that life begins at conception, but the real question that should be asked is this: If life doesn't begin at conception, then why do we have to kill it to get rid of it?

In a U.S. Senate committee, several different physicians and scientists testified about the fact that life begins at conception. One of those physicians was Dr. Jerome LeJeune, a professor of genetics at the University of Descartes in Paris. Dr. LeJeune discovered the chromosome pattern within Down syndrome. In Dr. LeJeune's testimony to the Judiciary Subcommittee, he stated, "After fertilization has taken place a new human being has come into being." He stated that this "is no longer a matter of taste or opinion," and it is "not a metaphysical contention, it is plain experimental evidence." He added, "Each individual has a very neat beginning, at conception." (176)

At the University of Pennsylvania, a physician by the name of Dr. Alfred M. Bongioanni affirmed:

> I have learned from my earliest medical education that human life begins at the time of conception... I submit that human life is present throughout this entire sequence from conception to adulthood and that any interruption at any point throughout this time constitutes a termination of human life... I am no more prepared to say that these early stages [of development in the womb] represent an incomplete human being than I would be to say that the child prior to the dramatic effects of puberty... is not a human being. This is human life at every stage. (177)

For years, "medical" abortions have been deemed a safe and trusted procedure. The Planned Parenthood website matter-of-factly asserts, "There are two ways of ending a pregnancy: in-clinic abortion and the abortion pill. Both are safe and very common." (178) It is interesting how often truth and lies get mixed up like a big casserole and served to the masses. Are abortions really safe? No, they are not. Are they common? Sadly, yes. That is the rotten truth.

There is absolutely nothing medical about abortion. Medicine is for treating an illness or injury. A "medical" abortion is the use of a chemical to kill a living being. If something is medicinal, it assists in curing a disease or relieving pain. Babies aren't diseases, and murdering them doesn't relieve pain. Dr. Bernard Nathanson, who helped found NARAL, narrated a twenty-eight-minute film called *The Silent Scream,* which showed an abortion of a twelve-week-old baby dying by aspiration abortion. He states, "We see the child's mouth open in a silent scream. This is the silent scream of a child threatened imminently with extinction." It is important to note that Dr. Nathanson had a change of heart later in life and lamented, "I am deeply troubled by my own increasing certainty that I had, in fact, presided over 60,000 deaths." Abortion is not healthcare, and a baby is not a disease. It is a human life that is protected under our United States Constitution. Abortion violates that baby's constitutional right to life.

The left has made the overturn of *Roe v. Wade* about removing a woman's "right to choose" and her "bodily autonomy." This is an old argument. Science has long proved that it is not her body. The baby is another human being with unique DNA belonging to the human genome. It is a human being made in the image of God, and to take that baby's right to life away not only is in defiance of our constitutional right to life, it denies God's perfect order and purpose for His creation.

A popular, fallacious assertion from the left is that Christians don't care anything about the needs of the mother or, after the baby's born, they don't step up to assist with the care of him or her. I decided to do some digging myself and compare Planned Parenthood with local pregnancy centers. Who is doing what? The National Library of Medicine website states, "A pregnancy center usually helps women with free pregnancy tests, ultrasounds, testing for sexually transmitted infections, and counseling on 'all options' for pregnancy. In addition, pregnant women are often offered resources such as maternity clothes, diapers, and parenting classes." To compare, the Planned Parenthood site states, "Planned Parenthood has provided lifesaving reproductive health care and empowered millions of people worldwide to make informed decisions to lead healthy, happy lives." (179) I couldn't locate any listing of materials afforded to mothers who choose life or post-abortion counseling offered to women who routinely experience a long list of side effects and trauma. Women who abort their babies are statistically 155% more likely to exhibit suicidal behavior. Does Planned Parenthood encourage women and men to stay abstinent until marriage? Wouldn't that be the safest way to prevent "unplanned pregnancies?" Oh, but that is not their agenda. It has never been their agenda.

Contrary to the left's blatant lies about pregnancy

centers and people of faith, statistics show that for every one Planned Parenthood, there are approximately fourteen pregnancy centers. America was founded on Judeo-Christian principles, including the fact that we are all created equally with God-given potential and the right to life, liberty, and the pursuit of happiness. It is our duty as citizens of this nation to protect those principles and rights.

The feminist movement has sold a pack of lies to women of all ages, swindling them out of the richness and beauty of God's design for them. The suggestion that women can only be successful if they terminate the life of their unborn child couldn't be more of a hoax. There is absolutely nothing empowering about *terminating* a life in order to *succeed* in life. It would be more honest to say that the termination of one life significantly impedes and burdens the second life. Remember the words of Dr. Fogel?

"The trauma may sink into the unconscious and never surface in the woman's lifetime... but a psychological price is paid. It may be alienation, it may be pushing away from human warmth, perhaps a hardening of the maternal instinct. Something happens on the deeper levels of a woman's consciousness when she destroys a pregnancy. I know this as a psychiatrist."

"Whoever causes one of these little ones who believe in Me to sin, it is better for him if a heavy millstone is hung around his neck and he is thrown into the sea." (Mark

9:42)

Do children rob adults of success? Do they burden men and women with unnecessary expenses? Isn't this idea purely materialistic and selfish? How base have we become? The left pushes the idea that not having kids will save you money; therefore, abortion is the solution to financial freedom. Better to drive a new car than raise a child; better to own a McMansion in the suburbs than to create a family to dwell in it. This is the philosophy that has permeated the minds of ignorant generations. However, statistics actually show that when a married couple has children, they have more drive and overall more focus in life.

Satan will do absolutely anything to destroy mankind, and he's been working on it since the Garden of Eden. The Old Testament records instances where worship to pagan gods included child sacrifice. Babies were placed over the fire, and the people would beat their drums loudly to drown out the screams! Abortion is modern-day child sacrifice. It is a sexual convenience and a blight on this nation. I submit to you that the fact that we had to overturn such an offensive law—*Roe v. Wade*—was a slap in the face to Almighty God, the Giver of life.

The United States of America was founded on the three principles of life, liberty, and the pursuit of happiness. In 1973, the decision made by the United States Supreme Court in the case *Roe v. Wade* made it legal to murder and take an innocent life in the womb. We have created an entire culture that devalues life. Truly, a man cannot love God and hate his brother. In essence, abortion is the hatred and devaluing of human life. After fifty-one years of legalized abortion in America, we have murdered seventy million children. Approximately 250,000 people die globally from gun violence/negligence per year, and approximately 40–50 million children die globally by abortion. This is staggering! It's no wonder why America is in jeopardy. Where is the remorse? Where is the outcry against this demonic injustice?

*** **TAKE A *CHANCE!*** ***

Research and discuss how figures like Margaret Sanger and organizations like Planned Parenthood influenced society's views on reproductive rights, often with underlying motives related to eugenics and population control. Explore the seemingly complex relationship between feminism, reproductive rights, and climate change narrative by researching the history of population control, discussing the ethical dimensions of abortion in your youth group, and exploring how political and cultural shifts affect women and families. By doing simple research and reflecting on both historical context and current perspectives of the "death industry," thoughtfully discuss the impacts of abortion since its official passing into law in 1973, understand its roots and impact on your parent's culture (GenXers or Millennials), and consider the value of life and family today.

"In a time of universal deceit,
telling the truth is a revolutionary act."

—Popularly (though Wrongly)
Attributed to George Orwell

Chapter 8
The Greatest Issue Facing America

Many believe this quote is attributed to George Orwell, the author of *1984*. Others say he never said it, nor did he ever write it. Regardless, it's how I feel about the topic of this chapter. Men, women, boys, and girls are so universally deceived that expressing biblical principles is sure to incite hatred and hot-tempered debates. A biblical worldview--seeing the world the way God sees it--is deficient in and outside of the church, and it's a shame.

Everything in our society is out of order. We have men wanting to be women and women wanting to be masculine like men. More and more children are being born into one-parent homes and many times are born out of wedlock. The divorce rate is at an all-time high and continues to rise. Less and less people are committed to getting married and having children than ever before. This is the pinnacle of Satan's goal to thwart God's command in Genesis 1:28. Our enemy, Satan, is destroying the family, and one of his most effective tactics is perverting male and female roles in society.

The fastest way to destroy a nation is to decimate the building block of the nation--the family. Every single issue we face in society is a result of the dismantling of the nuclear family, which is defined by the Bible as a monogamous relationship between one man and one woman for one lifetime. When a majority of the families in a particular society are fractured, you consequently reap a breakdown in a host of other areas. When people break, society breaks. When families falter, nations crumble.

But how do you break down the nuclear family? If you were the devil in 1620 America, how would you begin decomposing a society with strong, seemingly impervious biblical moorings? How would you begin to unravel the fabric of a citizenry who esteemed God's commandments in their state constitutions and fashioned their federal government to acknowledge that a Creator had endowed them with certain unalienable rights? I can tell you what I would do. I'd employ the same tactics of the serpent in the garden. I'd convince Adam to abdicate his responsibilities, I'd cultivate a lust for power in Eve, and I would undermine the Creator and His rules. Isn't that exactly what we're seeing today?

Satan has been pitting men and women against one another, and in turn, both genders have been abandoning our God-ordained roles found in the pages of the Bible. As a result, we have the most psychologically-confused generation of young people to ever walk this planet.

Last Chance

I used to get torn up about the fact that we, as Christians, allowed the government to take prayer out of public schools in 1962. But then I realized that the government didn't remove prayer from our school; we took Jesus and prayer out of the home. We left it up to the educational system and the government to raise our children. Men stopped guarding the gate. Women left the homes. The children suffered.

The family unit (one man, one woman, and children) is the first institution created by God. The first commandment God ever gave to Adam and Eve was to go and multiply (procreate) and populate the earth. Nearly every single talking point the left and the globalist elites are pushing defies that commandment from God. It is all about population control because the smaller the population, the easier it is to control. The self-governed family with a responsible father who provides for and protects his family, a nurturing mother who instills virtue into her children, and obedient children being trained to love God and seek first His Kingdom is the foundation--the building block--to a nation, and that is why it is so heavily under attack.

The world has a fluid definition of "family and marriage." It can be whatever that particular culture or person wants it to be. In other words, the family is whatever you want to call it. You can have it your way.

The idea of revising definitions of words and rejecting absolute truth is the religious belief of relativism. Truth is whatever you want it to be. If I say I am a hamburger, then I am a hamburger. If I say I am married to a fence post, then I am married to a fence post, and you must give me a marriage license. This preposterous philosophy has opened up a host of sodomite possibilities to be widely accepted in Western culture.

Another ingredient mixed into the assault on the traditional family comes from globalist elites pushing a false narrative. They wrongly suggest that bringing a certain amount of children into the world is selfish and burdensome to the planet. These fearmongers argue that the world is overpopulated and more children are causing this "climate crisis," which, of course, is a hoax. Climate change is called spring, summer, fall, and winter.

Regardless, we do not have the authority to play God by reducing the human population through vaccinations, abortion, contraception, and so forth. This is Satan's agenda to deceive people into playing God. God has commanded us in Genesis 1:28 to multiply and fill the earth. God is not worried about overpopulation; He is likely more concerned with the depravity of man.

Throughout history, it has been widely understood that sexual relations outside of the natural order prescribed by God are perversions (bestiality, pedophilia, fornication, abuse, adultery, sodomy, etc.). Participation in these acts is disobedience to God, harmful to oneself and others, and sinful. But as these laws which are antagonistic to God's laws are enacted in our nation, individuals stop feeling guilt for their debauchery. Sin is normalized. No one needs to feel ashamed because the government says our sin is perfectly acceptable! Legalizing abortion, the feminist movement, and same-sex marriage have seared the individual consciences of Americans. We have rejected God from our institutions; we have lost basic moral standards.

Breakdown of the Family as a Whole Through Communism

Why do they want to break down the family and confuse male and female roles? Because the fastest way to enslave, entrap, and control a nation is to break down the nuclear family. The left and global elites fear strong, biblical, structured families because they cannot control them. Why? Because they have principles and are united on those principles.

If you want to know God's original intent, you go to the Garden of Eden. It's there that we discover the first institution God created--the family consisting of Adam and Eve. Marriage is a covenant created by God between one man and one woman for life. Genesis 1:27 points out that when the two come together with God at the center, they become one union.

Notably, God's idea of marriage was incorporated into our nation's law, affirming that His idea of marriage was the clear path to success for any nation. In a bill introduced by Thomas Jefferson, James Wilson said, "By an act of the legislature of Pennsylvania, all marriages not forbidden by the law of God shall be encouraged." (180) The Texas Supreme Court in the case *Grigsby v. Reib* proclaimed:

> Marriage was not originated by human law. When God created Eve, she was a wife to Adam; they then and there occupied the status of husband to wife and wife to husband... The truth is that civil government has grown out of marriage... which created homes, and population, and society, from which government became necessary... [Marriages] will produce a home and family that will contribute to good society, to free and just government, and to the support of Christianity... It would be sacrilegious to apply the designation "a civil contract" to such a marriage. It is that and more--a status ordained by God. (181)

The lawmakers recognized that God's definition of marriage is good and holy, that society receives nourishment from its life-giving roots, and that anything outside of that is what creates confusion and chaos.

Today, children with two parents in the household are at an all-time low. According to the Pew Research Center, a study conducted in 2014 showed that 26% of children in America have a single parent, compared to only 9% in the 1960s. (182) Today, only 62% of children live with two parents in the house, whereas 87% of children had both mother and father in the house in the 1960s. Pew Research stated, "For decades, the share of U.S. children living with a single parent has been rising, accompanied by a decline in marriage rates and a rise in births outside of marriage." (183) Additionally, Pew did another study in the United States and 130 other countries which showed the U.S. having the highest rate of children living in single-parent homes. The statistics don't lie. We are harvesting the crop produced through years of skyrocketing divorce rates and illicit sex outside of marriage. Generations of impressionable boys and girls have been cheated out of growing up with a father in the home.

Statistics show that 70% of all prisoners come from a broken family and home life. (184) Additionally, children with divorced parents are twice as likely to do drugs, twice as likely to commit suicide, twice as likely to drop out of school, and 50% more likely to have health issues at a premature age.

One of our Founding Fathers, James Wilson, stated, "But of causes which are light and trivial, a divorce should by no means be permitted to be the effect. When divorces can be summoned... A state of marriage frequently becomes a state of war." (185) Our founders recognized that when laws and ideas in society make it easy to get divorced, preserving marriages becomes strikingly hard.

Truly, the family being under such attack in America reveals how much our country has been heavily influenced by communism and Karl Marx's poisonous ideas. Throughout many of Marx's writings, he describes the family unit as a form of "private ownership" that must be abolished. A man by the name of Robert Owen, known for his attempt in 1825 to fully implement his idea of a "utopian" society in New Harmony, Indiana, said: "I now declare, to you and to the world, that Man, up to this hour, has been, in all parts of the earth, a slave to a Trinity of the most monstrous evils that could be combines to inflict mental and physical evil upon his whole race. I refer to private, or individual property—absurd and irrational systems of religion—and marriage, founded on individual property combined with some one of these irrational systems of religion." (186)

In communism, the ways and methods may differ, but the goal of eliminating the idea of a traditional family between one man and one woman remains. In *Epoch Times's* book, *In the West*, "gender discrimination" is used as a weapon to maintain a state of "political correctness." In China, the "male chauvinism" label is used to provoke a similar destructive effect, though the specifics of its use differ. The gender equality advocated by Western feminism demands equality of outcome between men and women through measures such as gender quotas, financial compensation, and lowered standards. Under the CCP's slogan that women hold up half the sky, women are expected to show the same ability in the same work as their male counterparts. The root of this is Satan, the author of confusion.

Feminist Movement

I promise I will change your mind on this issue if you give me a few moments of your time. Although there are many factors contributing to the breakdown of the family, the greatest force, in my opinion, has been the feminist movement. An overwhelming percentage of Christians, in my experience, do not understand the damage the feminist movement has had on American culture. Most also do not understand that it spans at least 170 years of history.

During the 1960s and '70s, America started to see a large shift in the understanding of sex and male/female roles in society. This was largely due to the feminist movement. In the 1960s, it infiltrated America with what is known as the "sexual liberation/revolution" movement, also known as the second-wave of feminism. By and large, most people associate the feminist movement with equal rights, equal pay, or voting. Most people don't realize that the feminist movement did not give women the right to vote. The women's suffrage movement gave women the right to vote through the 19th Amendment of *The Constitution*, nearly fifty years prior to the feminist movement emerging.

The sexual liberation movement that occurred within the broader umbrella of the feminist movement (beginning in the mid-1960s) is similar to many of the early attempts of sexual liberation in some communist countries today. So-called "sexual liberation" was introduced in the name of "free love," meaning that any type of sexual activity should be permissible with zero restraints. Although there were many leaders across the world spearheading the "free love" movement, the first entrance of this movement into America was in 1953 with Playboy Magazine. Individuals like Alfred Kinsey, who played a large role in gender ideology seen in today's culture, also pushed the idea of "free love" in America by encouraging homosexual sex, "open marriages," and the concept of children having sexual desire. Fairly quickly, it became almost abnormal to be a virgin on your wedding night.

Betty Friedman, who was one of the main leaders of the second wave of feminism, published The Feminine Mystique in 1963. In it, she criticized the traditional family and set fire to the long-standing roles of men and women, declaring the notion that women are oppressed by the patriarchy. I believe it is also worth noting that Friedman was a radical socialist activist during her college years leading up into the 1950s. Betty was not only a member of the Young Communist League when she attended the University of California-Berkeley, she also requested to join the Communist Party USA twice.

If women already had the right to vote, then what was the purpose of the feminist movement? Feminism portrayed a perverted view of womanhood, claiming that the traditional view was oppressive. It offered a "liberating" bite from the fruit of the forbidden tree. "Take a bite, and you will be free!" its proponents cheered! "Patriarchy is oppressive!" they loudly exclaimed! "Women are equal to men!"

In truth, God has created the male and female and given them equal standing before Him. He doesn't prefer men to women any more than He prefers Jesus to the Holy Spirit. But while we are equal in righteousness as children of God, we are not equal in function. God created men and women for different purposes, and surrendering to the design found in the scripture brings peace and contentment. But rather than finding satisfaction in the perfect handiwork of God, the feminist movement blurred the lines and worked feverishly to paint a new, modern picture of "perfection." Sadly, it was nothing more than perversion. Instead of men and women working in harmony according to God's design (as seen in the garden), dissonance occurred. Women demanded equal rights and opportunities! Malcontent was sown into the psyche of the young and old by the leaders of the feminist movement. They claimed women needed "liberation" and "personal satisfaction" through a career and their own personal life apart from their family. They shouldn't be trapped in the home making meals, doing laundry, and rearing children when they could drop their infants off at day cares and find such liberation in their… cubicle. In reality, this bizarre lifestyle has only made women more unhappy and dissatisfied. Radical feminists knew that when divorce became easy (it was promoted as a means of liberating women), that would be when the family unit would crumble.

The feminist movement, propelled by the elites and the Rockefellers, argued that working women would equal more tax revenue. Furthermore, if women are working, their children will be placed in Rockefeller schools run by the government. At an early age, children are fed harmful propaganda, and parents unwittingly sanction the indoctrination and control of their children. Education, from preschool through college, is agenda-driven, producing liberal, hedonistic men and women whose minds have been brainwashed in a Marxist worldview.

Friedrich Engels suggested that in a communist society there would be no need to worry about where children would be placed since that would be the responsibility of the state. He wrote, "This removes all the anxiety about the 'consequences,' which today is the most essential social moral as well as economic factor that prevents a girl from giving herself completely to the man she loves. Will that not suffice to bring about that gradual growth of unconstrained sexual intercourse and with it a more tolerant public opinion in regard to a maiden's honor and a woman's shame?" (187) The end result of this logic is sexual promiscuity, which is a great way to break down a family. This is one of the goals in communism.

Nothing about the feminist movement has brought

gratification or familial prosperity to America. Some conservatives will suggest that the first wave of feminism was commendable, but modern feminism is what's rotten. Many have also equated the entire feminist movement with "women's rights," which, of course, is all a lie. What rights did women not have that men did in the '70s? They used very appealing and emotional verbiage to lure women into their snare. In reality, none of these newfound "rights" have delivered the emancipation and satisfaction that was promised. Instead, a country with broken-down families lies in its wake.

While the leaders of the movement tout "liberation," their use of this word begs the questions: What is the definition of liberation, and what does it entail? Progressives define liberation as being set free from limits on sex and gender roles. This flies in the face of the biblical definition of the term and countermands the Creator's design for males, females, and family government. Again, it's all an agenda that undermines God.

Once it becomes culturally acceptable for women to have sex with absolutely no consequences, you can develop an argument for why birth control and abortion is "necessary." The "liberation" that the feminist movement promoted was actually no promotion at all. It was a great big scam leading to sexual promiscuity, confusion, and pain. Above all, it was a rebellious rejection of God's perfect order for sex, marriage, and family. It was the beginning of a cultural acceptance of all types of sexual perversion. And now, having made it normal to have sex outside marriage for the sake of "liberation," we are drowning in the depths of depravity as the educational system teaches our children about sexual orientation and identity, grown men dance provocatively around children, and pedophiles are tolerantly called Minor Attracted Persons (MAPS). When you permit a level of moral turpitude and licentiousness, it will sooner rather than later become the new normal.

In relation to communism, the term "liberation" is a means of the destruction of traditional values and morality. For communists, the patriarchy of the biblical family is viewed as "oppressive" over women, and the idea of purity is viewed as a repression of human nature. The French socialist philosopher, Charles Fourier, who was called the "father of feminism," declared that marriage was oppressive and turned women into private property. The idea of "you will own nothing and be happy" is rooted in this philosophy. This all seems similar to the feminist movement. Communism encourages individuals to abandon tradition for the sake of "sexual liberation." Three words you hear thrown around quite often from the left today are "liberation," "love," and "freedom." If you investigate Karl Marx's writings, you will notice these words are sprinkled throughout them. This verbiage is frankly nothing more than a ploy to abandon tradition and morality. Sexual chaos is one of the key planks of the communist and Marxist ideology that facilitates the demise of the family.

The feminist movement groomed women to believe lies. "You can be just like a man!" "You can do anything that a man can do!" "You don't need a man!" "Patriarchy is oppression, and God is a bigot!" The feminist movement tried to prove that men and women are equal. But we are not equal. Of course, we are equal in value and dignity, but everything about men and women is different. Our physiology, our emotions, and our God-ordained roles in society are completely unalike. It's not a bad thing at all. It's a beautiful thing. Men are stronger, they're faster, and they are uniquely equipped to be leaders and protectors. Women have soft chests, they are more emotionally driven and compassionate, and they are called to be nurturers. This is not a "women need to get back to the kitchen and shut up" type of message. NO! What I'm saying is that women and men have different roles in society, and when we abandon those roles, society will suffer. Because the feminist movement tried to pit men against women and vice versa, now statistics show that women are the most unhappy and unfulfilled than any prior generation. We lack the fulfillment that comes from living contentedly in the role that God carved out for us. Because they have stepped outside the lane God designed for them to run in, women are unhappier than ever before.

Betty Friedman stated that women should pursue careers and higher education for "personal satisfaction." (188) Additionally, Germaine Greer, wrote that the "sexual repression of women prevented them from becoming personally fulfilled. But thanks to the pill and changing mores about sex outside of marriage, women could finally achieve the freedom and happiness that had been available to men for millennia." (189) The question that should be asked is whether or not the feminist movement actually benefited women as it claimed it would?

Women have traded their most valuable role within the nuclear family for 9-5 jobs that run them ragged. They are callously murdering their own unborn children and buying into hookup culture all in the name of "personal satisfaction." It's been reported by the National Center for Health Statistics that 1 out of 5 women aged 40-59 are on antidepressants. (190) The birth rate in the United States of America is plummeting each year, and it's estimated that by 2030, if we continue down this path, 45% of women ages 25-44 will be unmarried and childless. This is staggering when compared with statistics from 1980 when 65% of 25-year-old women were married. (191) Again, these repercussions came in the name of "personal satisfaction and my success." The feminist truly is all about me, me, me. This selfish attitude can be traced all the way back to the beginning in the book of Genesis when Eve was promised by the serpent that she would be even greater and better off than God Himself if she ate the fruit.

I do not deny that there are family situations where men abuse their leadership role as a husband and/or father.

There is nothing Christlike about abusing anyone, especially someone weaker and smaller than you, and I am not supporting and would never condone that behavior. The Bible teaches husbands to love their wives as their own flesh. It warns them not to provoke their children to wrath. And while it is true that all men are not exemplary in behavior, not all men are abusive. It is unnecessary to throw out the entire bushel basket of apples because you found one with worms. Discard the rotten apple and enjoy the good ones.

Prior to the feminist movement, Friedrich Engels, who was one of Karl Marx's closest friends, said that his ultimate hope was for America to have a widespread "unconstrained sexual intercourse" with the goal of eliminating traditional marriage and, above all, dissolving the family unit. (192) Today, the most well-known and active feminist group is the National Organization for Women (NOW). I would argue this group is the most anti-woman group in America. If you're looking to belong to a group which vehemently supports all access to abortion (even partial-birth abortions), advocates for LGBTQ "rights" (including men being allowed in women's bathrooms, sports, dressing rooms, etc.), and supports the worldwide legalization of prostitution, then this group is for you! I'd be remiss if I failed to mention that they also advocate for zero restrictions on pornography in libraries, they push for paid entitlement for family leave, complete access to abortions, affirmative action, government-funded (taxpayer-funded) daycare, and universal healthcare/insurance.

Masculinity

The feminist movement truly is a war on masculinity. Feminism has encouraged a hatred for men. It has blamed men for nearly every problem we are facing in society. Western civilization has pushed rugged masculinity aside and encouraged men to be passive, lazy, and effeminate. For decades, television programs have portrayed fathers to be oafs with no brains who are dependent upon others--especially their bossy, sharp-tongued wives whose primary goal is to mock them in front of their children.

The feminist movement pushes the idea that women can be independent and "don't need a man," which causes men to abdicate their role as leaders and start to become more feminine. Women have seized headship; men have become mild and submissive. Feminism widely embraces the term "toxic masculinity" to depict men who are strong, exert their maleness, and stand for truth and righteousness. However, what's actually toxic is weak men--men who run from evil and confrontation and allow women to assume headship. One of our Founding Fathers, Patrick Henry, said, "Adversity toughens manhood, and the characteristic of the good or the great man is not that he is exempt from the evils of life, but that he has surmounted them." (193) When men become passive, women instinctively become divisive and controlling.

Frankly, our world needs masculinity more than ever, especially in the household. One of the main tenets and goals of Marxism is to keep men as weak and docile as possible. Typically, women tend to be more emotionally led and men are more logical. The media primarily uses emotionally driven arguments as opposed to logical arguments, and women tend to fall for the emotional arguments. This is not misogynistic. This is a fact. Women do make the majority of their decisions based on their emotions. It goes all the way back to Genesis. Who ate the fruit? Eve. She was deceived--not Adam. But when God came walking into the garden after they sinned, He called for Adam. Why? Because Adam, the man (the leader and the protector), was not guarding the garden or her heart, and that is why Eve was deceived and made an emotionally driven decision. God's exclusive orders to Adam were to tend and "keep" the garden. The word "keep" is a military term. It means to guard as with a garrison. The cunning serpent should never have been allowed access to the garden to obfuscate the truth in Eve's mind. Adam wasn't being the leader God had called him to be. He failed. Men and women need one another. When a man and a woman come together with God at the center, they make a powerful team.

Have you ever noticed that the majority of the people who follow Dylan Mulvaney are women? Why? Because

The Greatest Issue Facing America

women are usually driven by their emotions rather than logic, "Aww, he identifies as a woman. I don't want to offend him or hurt his feelings." This is the exact reason why 76% of women supported the Democratic ticket in the last presidential election and around 58% of men voted Republican. (194) Men are to cover, lead, and cast a vision for their family. They must protect their wives and daughters from alluring deceptions that easily trick a compassionate heart.

If you've followed me for a while or listened to any of my speeches, you know that I don't like beta boys. However, I want you to really grasp what the difference between a beta boy and an alpha male is. Oftentimes, you hear an alpha male being described as someone that is muscular or buff-looking, but I would submit to you that being an alpha man has nothing to do with physical appearance, but rather how you lead. If you can lead and protect your family well and in the way God designed it, then I would consider you an alpha male. A beta boy, on the other hand, is a man that sees a fight and cowers or runs away. They lack courage. Our country needs alpha men that will stand in the face of evil and continue to speak the truth no matter how severe the persecution gets. If you're a strong, masculine male, take courage from Jesus. I can think of no greater example of an alpha male than Him.

> "If the world hates you, know that it has hated me before it hated you. If you were of the world, the world would love you as its own; but because you are not of the world, but I chose you out of the world, therefore the world hates you."
> (John 15:18-19, ESV)

In mid-2023, there were several videos that went viral from liberal women stating that they couldn't find any liberal masculine men and that all the masculine men they found were just misogynistic conservative men. Doesn't that prove the point that no woman—whether Christian, non-Christian, Democrat, or Republican—wants a beta soy boy that cannot get his hands dirty? What do women look for in romance movies? The weak, passive man? The one who sits on the sidelines? The one who allows the woman to pay for her food? The one who never takes a stand because he's too scared? Or do the women fall for the hero, the protector, the provider, the masculine man? Women want men who will fight for them, protect them, and lead them. They want men with blisters on their hands from real work, not from gaming on a Playstation in mommy's basement.

Men today are not being taught to be the men that God created them to be. Young boys have very few role models to help them embrace and appreciate manhood. Men are chastised by domineering women for being brawny, rugged, and heroic, and they are praised for wearing women's skinny jeans, lacking drive and testosterone, and talking like girls. How absurd! As a female, I will admit that women are partly to blame for this nonsensical gender confusion. The feminist movement, demanding equal opportunities, has subjugated men. The more women stepped into more masculine roles, the more men began caving to the feminist movement and have become more effeminate. This has made everything in society out of order. Women are kings, men are queens, and our children can choose their own gender. What a mess.

The agenda is applauded by the global elites because it drives a wedge between men and women and breaks down the family unit. A society of emotional women and emasculated men is easier to control.

LGBTQ

A man was allowed to participate in women's boxing at the 2024 Olympics in France. He punched his biologically female opponent, Angela Carini, so hard that she fell to the ground after two punches which occurred in less than fifty seconds. She couldn't take the blows. Where are the feminists who should be defending Carini? They're nowhere to be found because the feminist movement is what paved the way for gender ideology. Feminism, since the beginning, has advocated for LGBTQ "rights," for gender ideology in schools, and so forth. The feminists paved the way for the acceptance of sexual perversion of all kinds, by first culturally accepting sexual "liberation" for women.

The feminist movement has never been about protecting women. Instead, it has evolved into a movement led by sexual deviants marching for the sake of "women's rights" while murdering their own unborn children, defending men going into women's bathrooms and spaces, and grown men provocatively dancing in front of children. This cult is an ideology that is being backed by nearly every single institution in our society. And those who do not bow to this religious cult are silenced, suppressed, and made out to be hateful, homophobic bigots.

The cult takes those who are truly suffering from a real mental illness and confusion and uses them to promote an agenda that is ultimately all about population control. It is an abuse of people who truly may be suffering from mental illness. Progressive and globalist elites deem Christian morality to be oppressive. In reality, what is actually suffocating and destructive to society is the bondage of sin and the manipulation of individuals who are persuaded that they were born gay or are trapped in the wrong body.

The rainbow cult has played a huge part in dismantling the family unit. For instance, the legalizing of gay marriage in *Obergefell v. Hodges* truly devalued the nuclear family. Legitimizing gay marriage led to another evil form of child abuse--two gay men adopting children.

The Greatest Issue Facing America

In 1911, Leon Trotsky, a Soviet Union leader, wrote a letter to Vladimir Lenin in which he stated, "Undoubtedly, sexual oppression is the main means of enslaving a person. While such oppression exists, there can be no question of real freedom. The family, like a bourgeois institution, has completely outlived itself. It is necessary to speak more about this to the workers." (195) Lenin responded to Trotsky, writing, "And not only the family. All prohibitions relating to sexuality must be abolished... We have something to learn from the suffragettes: Even the ban on same-sex love should be lifted." (196)

Any individual who rejects the divine plan for human flourishing will undoubtedly suffer. Likewise, any nation which rejects the divine plan for human flourishing will suffer since nations are composed of individuals. Once we, as a nation, abandoned God's optimal plan for marriage, families began to fall apart. When families fall apart, nations fall apart. Make no mistake. This has always been an insidious agenda. Yes, it is a Marxist scheme, but above all, it is Satan's scheme. Collapse the family to control society. It has been Satan's agenda since the beginning of time in the Garden of Eden. The breakdown of the family is the result of very meticulous planning and the implementation of communism over the course of time in the United States. The devil is more patient than you will ever be.

STRONG FAMILIES = A STRONG SOCIETY

Something that is unfortunately very rarely talked about, specifically in the conservative movement, is how a free market, limited government depends greatly on strong families. It has been proven that when a society has more married parents (families), there is more economic prosperity. This includes the overall economic growth, a decrease in child poverty, and a higher median family income.

Why would the economy be better with both parents in the home? For one, it has been proven that men—on average—work harder, more diligently, and are more goal-oriented when they are married. Studies have actually revealed that married men typically work approximately 400 hours more and earn around $16,000 more per year compared to single men. A key reason why economic growth seems to soar when there are higher rates of married and fathering men is simply because being married motivated men in the labor force. (197) On the other hand, women are encouraged to decrease their hours of working outside the home or temporarily leave the workforce to focus on being a wife and mother. (198)

According to the Institute for Family Studies, "Strong families often serve as seedbeds for the kind of virtues—such as strong work ethic and the capacity for delayed gratification." (199) These are the qualities needed in order for a free market to thrive. Additionally, "Growing up in an intact, two-parent home makes children, especially boys, more likely to avoid disciplinary problems and stay on track in school." (200) In other words, when a country boasts robust families, that nation is more likely to be successful in a free market economy. Studies have also shown that as the rate of marriage decreased, the child poverty rate increased. Conversely, as the marriage rate has increased, the rate of child poverty has decreased. (201)

Over the past couple decades, America has seen an increase in divorces and more children being born into single-parent homes. Personally, I believe a large majority of this is due to the rise in secular individualism and the infiltration of communist ideas all throughout our institutions. In the 1950s, approximately 11% of children in America were born into a married home that later divorced. By 1970, that statistic had risen to nearly 50%.

In an article written by the *American Sociological Review*, the author noted how the family structure can affect economic outcomes in a slew of different ways and for various reasons: "Strong families can increase economic well-being because marriage and parenthood motivate men to work harder, more strategically, and more successfully, and to avoid behaviors—such as drinking to excess and criminal activity—that might limit their prospects at work." (202) It is also worth noting that when children are raised in stable, structured families with married parents, they are more likely to achieve a diversity in skills that will have a great impact on future opportunities. Robert Lerman pointed out that families with both parents at home are able to enjoy a higher level of income than those with single-parent families.

Two prominent economists, Isabel Sawhill and Robert Lerman, have revealed that the decline in marriages at a national level are linked to the increases in child poverty in America. In "For Richer, for Poorer...," Lerman points out that since the 1970s, the median family income in the United States has been rather stagnant. (203) This has been closely linked to the fact that more families are led by single parents. The link between the median family income and strong, two-parent families as a whole has been consistent and clear in the study conducted by the Institute for Family Studies. It revealed that states in the top percent of families with married parents have a higher median family income--nearly $2,600 more than those states with a lower percentage of families with married parents.

One of the greatest problems with the family is how the United States government is literally encouraging people to remain unmarried--especially those that are on a low-income budget. By and large, a single woman is able to receive more health benefits and welfare assistance if she is a single mother.

Strong families allow greater economic prosperity and provide children a significantly larger shot at living out the American Dream.

Disconnect from Parents

I've been asked a lot of interesting questions during my travels across the country, but there's one that has remained consistent: "What sparked this passion you have to stand for the truth?"

It all started within our home and with my upbringing. I appreciate my parents, who have raised me and my siblings in a home where we discussed the issues in our world. Since I can remember, we have spent a couple nights a week either watching the news, a documentary, or something with substance to get us thinking. It's important to note that we enjoyed these activities together.

Most families in our society are completely disconnected from one another. Everyone is on their phones constantly scrolling social media. The children have TVs in their rooms. Parents do not have their children's hearts anymore. Personally, I believe that's why so many young people lose their moral compass in college; the parents didn't have their hearts and didn't train them how to think biblically. Truly, your children will be educated by one of two things--the world or the Word of God. You, as the parent, will ultimately make that determination.

You must fight for your kids' hearts. Put away the unimportant distractions and teach them the why behind the what! In other words, don't just tell them what to do or what is right. Explain the principles behind what is right. Give them knowledge and understanding so they may walk in wisdom. My parents excelled at nurturing a relationship with me and my siblings. Instead of a host of cold, rigid rules, they fostered a beautiful family dynamic which inspired us all to want to keep those rules out of love and respect for our parents. I encourage you to make the time you spend together both fun and exciting so they look forward to talking with you about what's going on in the world.

> "Train up a child in the way he should go:
> and when he is old, he will not depart from it."
> (Proverbs 22:6, NIV, 1973-2011)

*** **TAKE A** *CHANCE!* ***

Explore how the breakdown of the nuclear family leads to societal problems, including higher rates of crime and poverty. Think about the consequences of abandoning traditional values, discussing why strong families are essential to a nation's health and freedom. Action steps can include researching family statistics, participating in discussions about the role of parents and marriage, and advocating for policies that strengthen family units.

"What has been will be again,
what has been done will be done again;
there is nothing new under the sun."

—Ecclesiastes 1:9 (NIV)

Chapter 9

How in the World Did We Get Here?

While nothing is new for God, we can say for certain that we are seeing things we've never seen before. Never before in human history have grown men been dressing as women, wearing makeup, and intruding into female spaces with half of society defending it and calling it normal and acceptable. This is unprecedented. Child sacrifice isn't new, but never before has a nation murdered over seventy million innocent unborn lives within fifty years. It's catastrophic and unnerving.

But how did we get here? How did we allow society to become so debased that we are questioning if there are only two genders, if children should cut off their healthy breasts and genitals, and if men should be entering women's spaces? How did we get to the place where we have a Supreme Court Justice, Ketanji Brown Jackson, who can't define what a woman is because she's not a biologist? We have a Health Secretary that was appointed to instruct us on our health, yet he is obese and thinks he is a woman. We have a sitting president that cannot even speak a full sentence. We are confusing right with wrong and calling evil good. The answer is simple. We've taken the freedoms and liberties we have for granted. We, as a country, have forgotten where our freedoms originated and lost sight of the hand of providence that got us here. Since we've taken the freedoms and liberties we have for granted, we have become a nation that has forgotten God.

Make no mistake that all of what is happening in the news, in the educational system, in the economy, in the military, and so forth is all a part of the agenda. This is the 2030 "you-will-own-nothing-and-be-happy" agenda, which will later give birth to a one-world government. A globalist oligarchy is the end goal for the elites. Some will call that statement conspiratorial, but don't take my word for it--take theirs. They are the ones pushing and calling for it, not me.

I firmly believe that the greatest threat to any society is the rejection of the One who created us--God Almighty. Thomas Jefferson said, "The God who gave us life also gave us liberty. How can the liberties of a nation be thought secure, when we have removed their only firm basis? A conviction in the minds of the people that these liberties are a gift from God." (204)

We have taken the freedoms and liberties we have for granted. All too quickly, we have surrendered the Judeo-Christian principles that made this nation so great. Freedom is a biblical idea--not an Islamic idea, nor a Hindu idea. It is a biblical idea. That is why America has enjoyed more freedom than any other nation in the history of our planet. The globalists' first target to take full control is to get America (the leading nation) to reject God. If we do not have a foundation on God, we will be easily deceived. This is why our nation has lost basic common sense standards; we have rejected God from nearly every single institution. Freedom only exists within the rule of law.

I heard a powerful quote a few years ago that I'll never forget: "Hard times create strong men, strong men create good times, good times create weak men, and weak men create hard times." This has been the cycle of events throughout history. Truly, the last time that we had strong, masculine men was in the 1940s when boys were so eager to fight for our country that they lied about their age. In the mid-1940s, men loved this country so much that they stormed the beaches of Normandy knowing they weren't going to make it home. Right now, we are in the era of weak men, and, if we don't rise up, we will be in hard times.

I believe one of the greatest contributing factors to the rejection of God from nearly every institution has been the idea that religion and politics are separate. Christian pastors have adopted this lie! You often hear, "Oh, that's too political!" or "Keep your religion out of politics!" However, politics and religion cannot be separated because God put them together. The entire Bible is government, family, and religion.

How in the World Did We Get Here?

Let me pose a few questions. Is abortion a political or spiritual issue? Is gay "marriage" a political or spiritual issue? Is the Second Amendment a political or spiritual issue? I submit to you that the ability to protect your family from a tyrannical government is both a spiritual and political issue. Satan, the author of confusion, loves that we have believed this lie that politics and religion are to be separate! While we think we are super spiritual because we are not addressing politics from the pulpit of our churches or in the workplace, Satan has infiltrated every facet of our society and perverted it. We have hidden our light under a bushel basket in the public square, and our pastors have failed to inculcate biblical truths in the hearts and minds of their congregations for fear of losing butts in pews and bucks in the offering plate.

Biblical truth is being attacked in the headlines every single day. You may disagree with me, but I'm going to drive this point home one more time. You cannot separate politics from religion because God put them together! And because we've believed this lie, the church has lost its voice, and the world is losing its mind. Everyone has a worldview, whether they are aware of it or not. When a person is choosing who to vote for at the polls, the decision is based on their spiritual and political worldview.

In an essay titled, "Memorial and Remonstrance Against Religious Assessments," James Madison wrote: "The religion then of every man must be left to the conviction and conscience of every man; and it is the right of every to exercise it as these may dictate. This right is in its nature an unalienable right. It is unalienable, because the opinions of men, depending only on the evidence contemplated by their own minds cannot follow the dictates of other men: It is unalienable also, because what is here a right toward men, it is a duty toward the Creator." (205)

Just as God raised up leaders like King David, Solomon, Joshua, Abraham, and so forth, He is also raising up leaders in our day to fight for righteousness, freedom, and truth.

There are questions that need to be pondered honestly by ministers and others alike. Are we influencing culture to be more like Christ, or is the culture primarily influencing the Christians? Are we, the ekklesia, bringing Christ into the public square, or is the United States government influencing the church to look and act more like the rest of the world? Jesus said we are "the salt of the earth." Have we lost our saltiness? If so, are we now good for nothing except to be thrown out and trampled underfoot?

As much as it pains me to say it, we are so worried about our 501(c)(3) status and the IRS coming after us that we won't even dare to talk about these common sense issues. We're so consumed by political correctness and not offending people in the congregation that we won't bring up the sanctity of life and the topic of abortion. Because we won't teach about basic biblical truth from the pulpit, this generation is the most biblically illiterate generation in history. Our religious leaders bow to the altar of fame and prize their role as "social media influencer" over speaking the truth. We've redefined truth and love, twisting scriptures to accommodate our feelings. Instead of the uncompromising message of repentance, we serve up gospel-lite and tout the idea that real Christians are jellyfish with no spine. A twenty-first century Christian must be compliant and accommodate all lifestyles and fetishes so that we are perceived as the kindest and gentlest people on earth. As a result, our ministers are gay, we celebrate transgenderism and social justice, and we reject the Ten Commandments. Words are redefined, passages of the Bible are either altered or ignored, and truth is altogether subjective. We are unrecognizable and pitiful.

Christian people will be tolerated as long as we never judge and love people for "who they are." Ironically, the people demanding acceptance and equal rights do not love themselves for who they truly are. I will accept them for who God created them to be, but I will not coddle their fairytale and assist in their quest to become someone they are not. Nurturing their fantasies is neither loving nor truthful. It is a betrayal of sound and sense. You cannot love someone without telling them the truth, since the terms love and truth are synonymous. Contrary to popular opinion, Jesus wasn't a weak, tolerant doormat who kept His opinions to Himself.

Without submission to the Creator of morality, you

cannot have a moral society. You may be able to sustain it for a period of time, but that society will still collapse in the end. This is what has happened all throughout human history. Every nation overcome with evil has been destroyed; it rotted from the inside out.

After you get a society to reject God, you then have to break down the foundation of society--the family. The Communists fear strong, godly, structured families because they cannot control them. This is why the family unit between one man and one woman is constantly under attack. In order to conquer a civilization, you must conquer the building block. If you trace back through American history, the major step to breaking down the family was the feminist movement, largely funded by the Rockefellers and many others who have their hands in the World Economic Forum/World Health Organization. Through the feminist movement, they capitalized on emotion, suggesting that women could not be truly satisfied and fulfilled without a career outside the home. They advertised a shiny new identity that was sure to bring joy to every female.

Thomas Jefferson, one of our Founding Fathers, stated, "For a well informed society is the best defense against tyranny." (206) This statement couldn't be more true. It explains why the "conservative" town I'm from (Murfreesboro, TN) has had pride parades and allowed men posing as women to enter women's bathrooms. Public ignorance is why pornographic books have been placed in several school libraries here in Rutherford County. People are oblivious to what is happening. We have been completely apathetic, we've been complacent, and, quite frankly, we've been cowards. While our communities are infiltrated with immorality, we sit around like the blind religious leaders and the Pharisees, naively thanking God that "Tennessee isn't like California." While we're over here with our heads in the sand, thanking God we're not like them, Satan is having a heyday getting his hands into every remaining vestige of godliness, including a medical facility that is topping the charts in performing gender mutilation surgeries on minors.

GK Chesteron said, "Tolerance is the virtue of a man with no conviction." (207) Whenever I speak in Tennessee, I always make sure to remind the crowd that if we don't take a firm and vigilant stance on biblical principles, we will be just like California in less than ten years!

What we are facing in the early twenty-first century with the silencing, the oppression of masks, the censorship from Big Tech is all textbook Marxism. The Heritage Foundation published an article on Marxism stating:

> The United States has successfully confronted Marxist attempts to derail it from its historic path of liberty and order. The multifaceted effort to defeat the enemy, generally referred to as the Cold War, concentrated many of the best minds in the country. In 1991, when the Soviet Union dissolved, many Americans and oth-

ers around the globe justifiably believed that communism had been defeated. However, American Marxists, making use of the complacency that victory often produces, have gained more influence than ever before. Cloaking their goals under the pretense of social justice, they now seek to dismantle the foundations of the American republic by rewriting history; reintroducing racism; creating privileged classes; and determining what can be said in public discourse, the military, and houses of worship. Unless Marxist thought is defeated again, today's cultural Marxists will achieve what the Soviet Union never could: the subjugation of the United States to a totalitarian, soul-destroying ideology. (208)

One of our Founding Fathers, John Adams, constantly correlated virtue with freedom and expressed that if America did not remain a virtuous nation, we would not have true liberty. Essentially, if we do not have morality in our society, we will lose our freedoms and rot from the inside out.

In *The Federalist Papers*, James Madison wrote:

> As there is a degree of depravity in mankind that requires a certain degree of circumspection and distrust, so there are other qualities in human nature that justify a certain portion of esteem and confidence. Republican government presupposes the existence of

these qualities in a higher degree than any other form. Were the pictures that have been drawn by the political jealousy of some among us faithful likeness of the human character, the inference would be, that there is no sufficient virtue among men for self-government: and that nothing less than the chains of despotism can restrain them from destroying and devouring one another. (209)

When Alexis de Tocqueville came to America, he was astonished at how the country was thriving and flourishing. After he arrived back in France, he wrote his observations in his book, *Democracy in America*. Among many other profound statements encompassing the rationale for America's exceptionalism, Tocqueville resolutely asserted, "Liberty cannot be established without morality." (210)

*** TAKE A *CHANCE!* ***

Learn how moral foundations, strong leaders, and religious influence once guided society and consider how apathy has allowed harmful ideologies to take root. Examine the connection between faith, family, and national strength, reflecting on the cyclical rise and fall of civilizations. Journal about faith in politics, and creating presentations on how strong families build strong nations.

Epilogue
My Message to Generation Z— Saving Our Republic

★★★

I am often asked why I take a stand. The first reason I choose to be outspoken is because truth is truth no matter your age, your background, or your skin color. Objective truth applies to everyone. Secondly, you will spend your time on whatever you're passionate about. I want to protect our freedoms, and I also want the generations to come to experience the constitutional freedoms afforded to us by the founders. Most importantly, complacency is a disgrace to the men and women who have served in our armed forces, sacrificing to defend and protect this nation from regimes seeking to overthrow it. Thousands of honorable men and women have paid the ultimate price so that we could enjoy the freedoms and liberties found only in America. Men stormed the beaches of Normandy knowing they were about to die, and we are too lazy to vote? We aren't even willing to suffer a little persecution in order to stand for basic truth?

Ronald Reagan gave his Gubernatorial Inaugural Address in 1967, and he offered some convincing thoughts we should never forget: "Perhaps you and I have lived too long with this miracle to properly be appreciative. Freedom is a fragile thing, and it's never more than one generation away from extinction. It isn't passed through by inheritance; it must be fought for and defended constantly by each generation, for it comes only once to a people. And those in world history who have known freedom and then lost it have never known it again." (211)

Freedom is not just given; it takes work, and it comes with responsibility. If we aren't willing to do the bare minimum and speak the truth, then who will?

When I think of my generation, Gen Z, I think of William Bradford, whom I mentioned earlier in this book. Bradford was a young man of courage and humility. At the age of sixteen, he was faced with a decision that would change his life forever--follow Christ and be disowned by his family, or reject Christ and remain comfortable with his family. William Bradford chose Christ. He chose the uncomfortable, unpopular road--to be rejected by his family. As a teenager, Bradford understood that the price of rejecting Christ was far more expensive than the cost of being disowned by those around him. One produced temporary discomfort; the other brought eternal consequences that could not be altered. Bradford went on to be one of the prominent leaders of the Mayflower, playing an enormous role in the religious freedom we enjoy today. I believe more young people like William

Bradford will rise up amidst this hot political climate and stand for the truth. This is a battle for the souls of the nation.

We are constantly blaming another generation for our current problems (myself included). We say, "If that generation would have stood then, we wouldn't be here now!" And while this may be true to an extent, it is time that we take responsibility, stop playing the victim, and take action. We do way too much complaining in America. I believe there are three basic steps to see success--a dream, a vision, and action. Everybody dreams. Some envision the steps to attain that dream. Very few take action upon those steps. But those who act are the ones who create change. Dale Carnegie said, "Inaction breeds doubt and fear. Action breeds confidence and courage. If you want to conquer fear, do not sit home and think about it. Go out and get busy." The moral of the story is that we have to stop complaining about the things happening in our country and do something about them!

Gen Z, you have been fed lies. You and I have been told that if we want to be successful, we should act, talk, and live like the rest of the world. Big Pharma has deceived us into believing that if we have depression, we need medication to fix it. If we have ADHD or anxiety, we need to be medicated. If we are obese and struggle with our health/weight, we need Ozempic or a pill to fix it. Women have been told if they struggle with acne or hormonal issues, they need birth control. The list goes on and on.

We have been lied to by nearly every institution in our society.

Generation Z is really the first generation to have full access to cell phones, social media, technology, etc. Unfortunately, we haven't been properly equipped to face these advancements and combat the lies that accompany them. We have been told to sit down, be quiet, and not ask questions. I believe this is a huge reason why we are here as a culture. We don't ask enough questions. What does this piece of legislation mean? Why are they putting that into place? What are the ramifications of that city council's decision? If you are in a classroom and the teacher says something about our history that is inaccurate, question it and begin a healthy dialogue about it. Rise up and speak out! This is a call to action!

Pursue what you are passionate about. Get involved! Know your state representatives, school board members, senators, etc. Participate with your local school board, city council, and local conservative groups. There are tons of amazing organizations (two of the ones I've done extensive work with are Concerned Women for America and Turning Point USA) doing so much for America. Are there specific issues that resonate with you? Join groups that address them! Imagine the impact that could be made if hundreds of dedicated people showed up to work toward educating the public, challenging liberalism, and financing biblical candidates and issues. What would happen if Gen Z awoke from their slumber and mustered the courage and motivation to speak out?

Once you locate your passion and begin participating, you need to dress like you care. Don't show up in pajamas, yoga pants, or low-cut, tight tops that expose your cleavage, ladies. Guys, put on a tie and tuck in your shirt. This may seem simple or silly, but it can immediately cause professionals to either quickly dismiss you or take you seriously. Together, we can Make America Classy Again.

After you isolate an issue you're passionate about, study it. Read books. We must educate ourselves. If you cannot defend what you're standing for, what use is it? As stated by many of our founders, if we do not understand our past or history, we should expect to repeat it. We must recognize and appreciate the price that was paid to secure our freedoms and learn why the founders pledged their lives, their fortunes, and their sacred honor. A personal sacrifice of such grand proportions must have been weighed with intense contemplation. What produced such valor and selflessness?

In order to defend any kind of evil, you must be able to identify right vs. wrong. I would highly recommend taking a worldview test in order to assess your own spiritual fitness. Do you think like a Marxist? Are you a Christian who actually behaves like a socialist? You might be surprised. A worldview test will renew your mind with a biblical perspective and help you think and act in accordance with God's Word. This is of utmost importance. In a day when words like "justice" are being redefined, you must be sure that you possess the biblical interpretation. Find a church which is faithful to orthodox Christianity and a pastor bold enough to teach about sin, abortion, homosexuality, etc. Attend consistently, support the vision of the church, and immerse yourself in the Word of God. The last thing we need is to mobilize "Christians" who land on the wrong side of the issues because they don't know how to rightly divide the Word of truth.

Additionally, we must participate in elections. The amount of Christians I have met who do not vote is disgusting and discouraging. It is our duty, just as it was in biblical times, to pay attention to what is happening around us and let our light shine. We will never see "righteousness exalt a nation" if we aren't willing to be a voice for righteousness. Participation is not optional! Our vote is an important factor in determining whether our nation will be blessed or cursed by God. When God gives us something, He expects us to steward it and use it for His glory. When we, as Christians, choose not to participate in the voting process or proclaim that we do not care about politics, we have blood on our hands. Whether we realize it or not, we are declaring that the seventy million innocent lives that have been murdered in the womb isn't our problem––that the thousands upon thousands of children's lives being destroyed through genital mutilation isn't our problem. It is our problem if we love our neighbors. It has everything to do with us. You may not want to be involved in politics, but politics sure wants to be involved with you, your family, your church, etc. Your piety will come to a screeching halt when the government inevitably threatens to take your property, your right to privacy, or your religious freedom. COVID-19 and mandatory vaccinations were just practice. It is our duty as Christians to vote biblically.

Above all, seek and honor the Lord in all that you do. Give God preeminence in all things. Consider these verses:

> "How can a young person stay on the path of purity? By living according to your word. I seek you with all my heart; do not let me stray from your commands. I have hidden your word in my heart that I might not sin against you." (Psalm 119:9-11, NIV)

This is not just a political battle we are up against; this is a spiritual battle between good and evil. We will never end this chaos if we do not take a bold and vigilant stance on these issues. One of my favorite passages in scripture is from Isaiah when he heard the Lord say, "Whom shall I send? Who will go for us?" Isaiah replied, "Here I am, Lord. Send me!" (Isaiah 6:8, NIV)

Will you go? Will you stand and be counted? Will you consider it an honor and privilege to suffer in the name of Jesus Christ? David seemed ill-equipped and inexperienced. He was just a kid bringing lunch to his older brothers. The intimidating size of Goliath's frame combined with his thunderous taunting should have driven this immature shepherd boy to cower in fear with the rest of the Israelite army. But living inside this small boy's heart was simple faith in a big God. Apart from God, David could do nothing.

But when David yielded to God Almighty, his size was of little consequence. What about you? Will you cower like the majority of the Israelite army, or will you join the ranks of lionhearted men like David who pledged to overthrow the God-defying, demonized giant who defied the living God?

It is our duty as Christians to be bold and courageous—to speak the truth in love because love without truth is hypocrisy. You cannot have one without the other. It's time for us to be courageous like Josiah and Daniel. Outnumbered, they stood fearlessly and adhered to the law of God no matter how intense the persecution became.

We are all going to stand before God at the judgment seat one day, and He's going to ask us what we did when it was our turn. I want to encourage you, regardless of your age, to hold fast to this quote from John Adams. He said, "Always stand on principle, even if you stand alone!" (212) If you are the only person in the room standing for the truth, keep standing! Never waver!

In the opening pages of this book, I mentioned a quote from Ben Franklin. He said, "You have a republic, if you can keep it!" (213)

Let's make this personal. As an American citizen who

has inherited unalienable rights and freedoms, how are you personally maintaining our republic? If everyone behaved exactly like you, would our republic be in jeopardy? Are you willing to do what it takes to help restore and preserve the United States of America? Will you rise up and protect her from dangerous ideologies and unbiblical philosophies? Do you recognize the God-hating agenda that seeks to sterilize our youth, murder the unborn, indoctrinate our children, and euthanize our elders? What are you willing to do about it? May we all have eyes to see and ears to hear!

"We the People" must become fed up with the lies, the fear-mongering, and the manipulation from the globalist elites. The only thing that is preventing these billionaires from taking complete control is "We the People"--little ole you and me. If you are not standing in the way of their agenda, restraining the tidal wave of evil, start today. This may be America's last chance. Never give an inch! Stay in the fight! Take courage, freedom fighters! God bless you, and God bless the United States of America!

Acknowledgments

First and foremost, I want to thank my Lord and Savior, Jesus Christ, for prompting me to take action, guiding me through this entire journey, and keeping me humble and steadfast.

I am deeply grateful to my parents for their unwavering support. They encouraged me to push through the writing process, even when it meant sleepless nights and staying home for days on end. Thank you for being patient with me, even with all my crazy ideas. I wouldn't be who I am today if not for my parents.

To my amazing siblings, Izzy, James, and Sarah: thank you for your steadfast support and your love for God and country. I'm beyond blessed to have each of you in my life.

To my grandparents, thank you for your prayers, words of advice, and encouragement.

General Flynn has been there since the very beginning. At 15, he took a chance on me and allowed me to speak at my first ReAwaken America Tour. He is one of the most genuine and kind-hearted individuals I've met in this movement, and I am extremely grateful for his support.

Turning Point USA began my journey in the fight for freedom. From starting a TPUSA chapter at 13 to organizing the first Teens Against Gender Mutilation rally at 15, this organization has been transformative. Charlie Kirk has truly created a movement of world-changers.

Young Women for America (YWA) is hands-down the greatest women's organization (not that I'm biased!). Since joining in 2022, I've experienced the incredible sisterhood within YWA, something rare and invaluable. YWA's leaders are modern-day Esthers and Deborahs, standing for truth and Biblical values in a world that has largely turned away from God.

To the Alexandroni family, thank you for pouring into me since I first met you all. I will never forget the words of wisdom, knowledge, and encouragement you all have given me.

Thank you to Felix Strategies for believing in me throughout the writing and podcasting process. I could not have done it without you.

Finally, I want to thank each and every American patriot for fighting to protect this Republic. This is not about fame, popularity, or money. It is about freedom. It is about protecting our God-given rights.

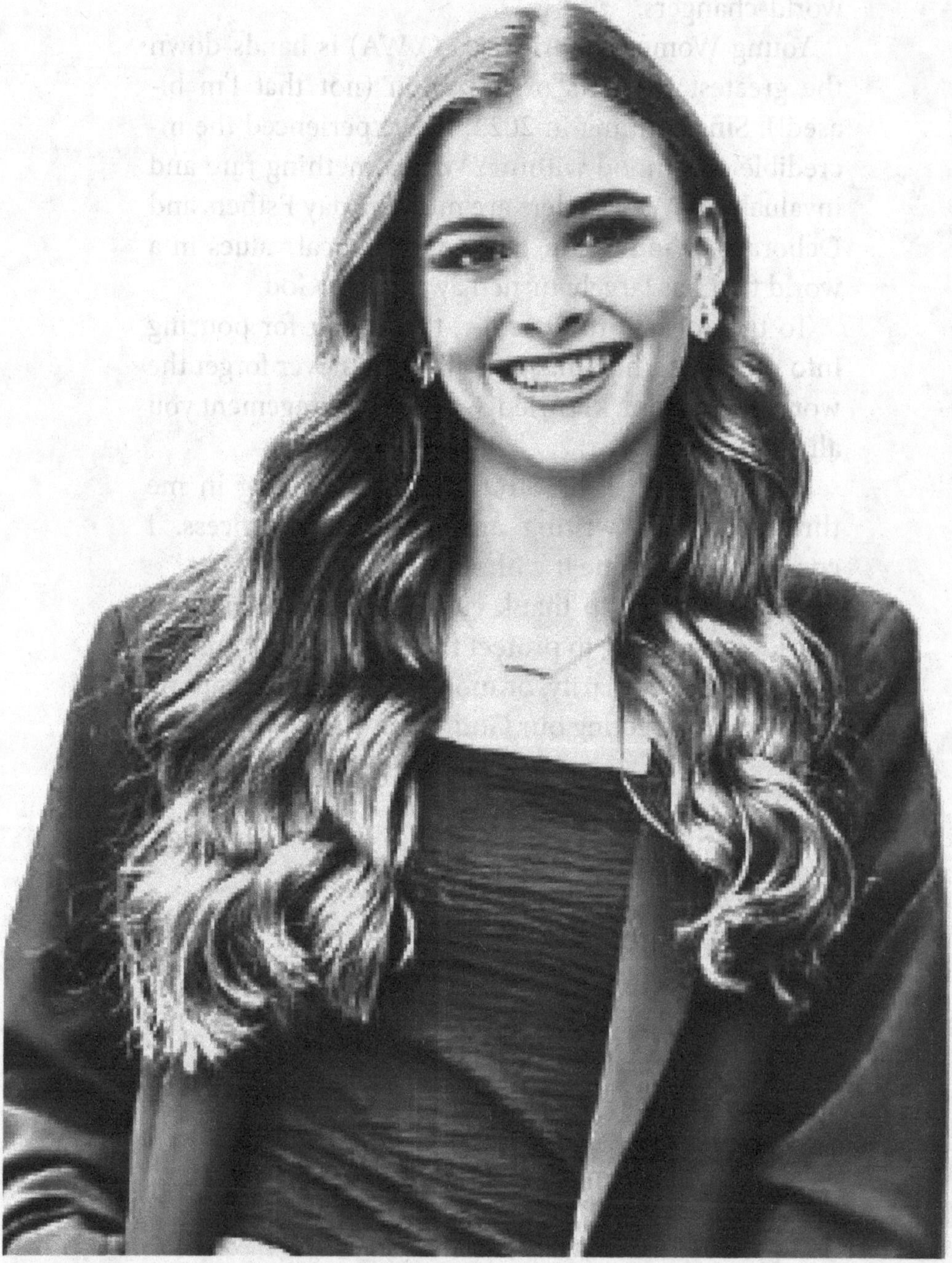

About the Author

HANNAH FAULKNER, at just 17 years old, is one of the most dynamic young voices on the American patriot landscape. Known for her fearless approach and unshakable principles, Hannah travels the nation, engaging thousands of patriots with powerful, truth-driven insights into today's most pressing issues. As the founder of Culture of 1776, Hannah leads a mission to ignite the next generation with a renewed sense of courage and common sense in a society where these virtues are often overlooked.

Through her podcast, *The Hannah Faulkner Show*, she not only unpacks complex topics but also equips her audience with the tools they need to make informed decisions and stand firm in their values. Whether she's on the road speaking to packed audiences or behind the mic on her show, Hannah embodies the spirit of a new patriotism, inspiring others to take a bold stance and rekindle the spirit of 1776 for the next generation.

About the Author

HANNAH FAULKNER, at just 17 years old, is one of the most dynamic young voices on the American patriot landscape. Known for her fearless approach and unshakable principles, Hannah travels the nation, engaging thousands of patriots with power and truth-driven dialogue on the most pressing issues. As the host of the podcast 1776, Hannah leads a mission to inspire her generation with a renewed sense of courage and common sense in a society where these virtues are often overlooked.

Through her podcast "The Hannah Faulkner Show," she not only unpacks complex topics but also equips her audience with the tools they need to make informed decisions and stand firm in their values. Whether she's on the road speaking to packed audiences or behind the mic on her show, Hannah embodies the spirit of a new patriotism, inspiring others to take a bold stance and rekindle the spirit of 1776 for the next generation.

Citations

Chapter 1

1. Marcus B. Huish, The American Pilgrim's Way in England. (London: The Fine Art Society, 1907), 105.

2. Francis Newton Thorpe, ed., The Federal and State Constitutions Colonial Charters, and Other Organic Laws of the States, Territories, and Colonies Now or Heretofore Forming the United States of America (Washington, D.C.: Government Printing Office, 1909).

3. David Barton, The Founders' Bible (Mercury Ink, 2012).

4. Alexis De Tocqueville, "Chapter 22: How the American Democracy Will Continue to Develop," Democracy in America, Project Gutenberg, published 1840; last modified February 1997, https://www.marxists.org/reference/archive/de-tocqueville/democracy-america/ch22.htm.

5. Krishan Kumar, "The Origins and Character of American Exceptionalism," The Journal of American History 99, no. 4 (2013): 1247-1261, https://www.

jstor.org/stable/10.1086/664595.

6. Barton, The Founders' Bible.

7. Carson Choate, "POLL: Only 16% of Gen Z Adults are Proud to Live in the US," Daily Wire, January 10, 2023, https://dailycaller.com/2023/01/10/morning-consult-poll-genz-proud-america/.

8. Barton, The Founders' Bible.

9. Norbert Compagna, "Virtue in Tocqueville's America," Amerikastudien / American Studies 52, no. 2 (2007): 169-186, https://www.jstor.org/stable/41158302.

10. TBA.

11. Aldous Huxley, Brave New World Revisited (New York: Harper & Brothers, 1958), 62.

12. New American Standard Bible online, published 1960; last modified 2020, https://www.biblegateway.com/verse/en/Galatians%205%3A13.

13. An American Dictionary of the English Language, Noah Webster (18th Printing, 1995), s.v. "Theocracy, N."

14. "Chief Justice Earl Warren on Equal Education and the Guiding 'Good Book,'" Our Lost Founding, May 17, 2019, https://ourlostfounding.com/chief-justice-earl-warren-on-equal-education-and-the-guiding-good-book/.

15. "United States vs. Macintosh, 283 U.S. 605," Supreme Justia, 1931, https://supreme.justia.com/cases/federal/us/283/605/.

16. Donald S. Lutz and C. S. Hyneman, "The Relative Influence of European Writers on Late Eighteenth-Century American Political Thought," The American Political Science Review 78, no. 1, (1984): 189-197, https://www.jstor.org/stable/1961257.

17. William Bradford, Of Plymouth Plantation, 1620-1647, ed. Samuel Eliot Morison (Knopf, 1952).

18. C. B. Galloway, Christianity and the American Commonwealth (American Vision, Inc., 2005), 143.

CHAPTER 2

19. John Heitzenrater, "Toward a New Political Science: Reflections on the Point of Departure in Tocqueville's Democracy in America," Netcrit, November 8, 2013, https://www.netcrit.com/history/reflections-

on-the-point-of-departure-in-democracy-in-america.

20. Heitzenrater, "Toward a New Political Science."

21. Roger Williams, Rhode Island Charter, 1663 (Rhode Island State Archives, 1663), https://docs.sos.ri.gov/documents/civicsandeducation/teacherresources/RI-Charter-annotated.pdf.

22. Eric Metaxas, If You Can Keep It: The Forgotten Promise of American Liberty (Viking, 2016), retrieved from https://ericmetaxas.com/books/if-you-can-keep-it/.

23. "The Constitution of the United States," The Library of Congress, 1787, https://www.loc.gov/item/2021667573/.

24. "Chicago Fines Churches for Holding Services in Violation of Statewide Lockdown Order," Fox News, May 20, 2020, https://www.foxnews.com/politics/chicago-fines-churches-violation-statewide-lockdown-order.

25. J. B. Pritzker (@GovPritzker), "April Hosts Many Important Celebrations for Some of the Largest Religions…," X (formerly Twitter), April 12, 2020, https://twitter.com/GovPritzker/sta-

tus/1249427348069416960.

26. "Chicago Fines Churches...," Fox News.

27. "Loving Your Neighbor by Wearing a Face Mask," Raising Everyday Disciples (blog), 2020, https://raisingeverydaydisciples.com/loving-your-neighbor-by-wearing-a-face-mask/.

28. "Masterpiece Cakeshop, Ltd. v. Colorado Civil Rights Commission, 584 U.S. ___," Supreme Justia, 2018, https://supreme.justia.com/cases/federal/us/584/16-111/.

29. Erwin Chemerinsky, "Not a Masterpiece: The Supreme Court's Decision in Masterpiece Cakeshop v. Colorado Civil Rights Commission," American Bar Association, https://www.americanbar.org/groups/crsj/publications/human_rights_magazine_home/the-ongoing-challenge-to-define-free-speech/not-a-masterpiece/.

30. "303 Creative LLC v. Elenis, 600 U.S. ___," slip op. at 23, 2023 (Gorsuch, J., concurring), https://www.supremecourt.gov/opinions/22pdf/21-476_c185.pdf.

31. "303 Creative LLC v. Elenis," 2023.

32. "303 Creative LLC v. Elenis," 2023.

33. Penny Nance, "Penny on CBN: Religious Freedom at Stake," Concerned Women for America, July 27, 2022, https://concernedwomen.org/religious-freedom-at-stake/.

34. "Gadsden flag," historical flag used by Commodore Esek Hopkins, the United States' first naval commander in chief, as his personal ensign during the American Revolution (1775–83)," Britannica.

35. Mark A. Kellner, "British Pro-Life Advocate Again Arrested for 'Thoughtcrime' of Silent Prayer Near Abortion Clinic," Washington Post (Washington, D.C.), Mar. 6, 2023.

36. J. Smith, "Elderly Woman Convicted Under FACE Act for Protesting at Abortion Clinic," Justice.gov, August 13, 2024,https://www.justice.gov/usao-dc/pr/final-defendant-sentenced-federal-civil-rights-conspiracy-and-freedom-access-clinic

37. Lila Rose (@LilaGraceRose), "At the Age of 74, Joan is Facing Up to a Decade in Prison…," X (formerly Twitter), September 8, 2023, https://x.com/LilaGraceRose/status/1703884099331498121.

38. "Paula Scanlan on Media Pressure and Team Dynamics at the University of Pennsylvania," Independent Women's Forum, July 22, 2024, https://www.iwf.org/female-athlete-stories/paula-scanlan/.

39. "Paula Scanlan on Media Pressure…," Independent Women's Forum.

40. David Limbaugh, Persecution: How Liberals Are Waging War Against Christianity (Regnery Publishing, 2003)

41. "U.S. Department of Health and Human Services," A statement by U.S. Department of Health and Human Services Secretary Kathleen Sebelius, January 20, 2012, [Press release], retrieved from https://www.hhs.gov/news/press-releases/2012/01/20/a-statement-by-u-s-department-of-health-and-human-services-secretary-kathleen-sebelius.html.

42. Justin Cooper, "FBI, Social Media Met Weekly to Censor Americans Before 2020 Election: MO AG," American Military News, December 2, 2022, https://americanmilitarynews.com/2022/12/fbi-social-media-met-weekly-to-censor-americans-before-2020-election-mo-ag/.

43. "Defending Election Integrity, AG Jeff Landry Calls for Repeal of Biden Executive Order," L'Observateur (LaPlace, LA), Sept. 28, 2022.

44. Yuri Bezmenov, Deception Was My Job, Free-World Press, 1984, lecture, 2:15:15.

CHAPTER 3

45. "The Bill of Rights: A Transcription," National Archives and Records Administration, 1789, https://www.archives.gov/founding-docs/bill-of-rights-transcript.

46. Deborah Avant, "From Mercenary to Citizen Armies: Explaining Change in the Practice of War," International Organization 54, no. 1 (2000): 41-72, https://www.jstor.org/stable/2601317.

47. "Natural Law," Wikipedia, October 11, 2024, https://en.wikipedia.org/wiki/Natural_law.

48. Thomas Aquinas, "Summa Theologiae," New Advent, 2017, https://www.newadvent.org/summa/.

49. Frédéric Bastiat, "The Law," Online Library of Liberty, 1850, https://oll.libertyfund.org/title/bastiat-the-law

50. David B. Kopel and Vincent Harinam, "Britain's Failed Weapons Control Laws Show Why the Second Amendment Matters," Cato Institute, August 28, 2018, https://www.cato.org/commentary/britains-failed-weapons-control-laws-show-why-second-amendment-matters.

51. "The Chinese Civil War: The Rise of the Communist Party and Mao Zedong," Asia for Educators, accessed October 23, 2024, https://afe.easia.columbia.edu/special/china_1900_mao_war.htm."

52. "Bureau of Alcohol, Tobacco, Firearms and Explosives," National Firearms Act | Bureau of Alcohol, Tobacco, Firearms and Explosives, U.S. Government Printing Office, June 26, 1934, https://www.atf.gov/firearms/national-firearms-act.

53. John Ross, Unintended Consequences, (Accurate Press, 1996), 103.

54. Firearms and Violence: A Critical Review, eds. Charles F. Wellford, John V. Pepper, and Carol V. Petrie (The National Academies Press, 2005), PAGE NUMBER, https://doi.org/10.17226/10881.

55. The Effectiveness of Federal Gun Control Laws: An Assessment of the 1994 Assault Weapons Ban,

(Office of Justice Programs, 2004), 3.

56. Joe McNamara, "The Reality of Gun Violence," Kansas City Star (Kansas City, MO), Sept. 22, 1992.

57. The Myth of Thomas Jefferson and Gun Control (Historical Press, 2021), 87.

58. "Extreme Risk Protection Orders: A Legal and Policy Review," National Conference of State Legislatures, 2020, https://www.ncsl.org/research/civil-and-criminal-justice/extreme-risk-protection-orders.aspx.

59. "Covenant School Shooter's Manifesto Revealed," New York Times (New York City, NY), Apr. 20, 2023.

Chapter 4

60. Saul D. Alinsky, (1971). Rules for Radicals: A Pragmatic Primer for Realistic Radicals (Vintage Books, 1971), PAGE NUMBER.

61. Klaus Schwab, "This Is What The WEF Is All About," YouTube, May 3, 2016, video, 15:59, https://www.youtube.com/watch?v=EFl_V9tEYm0.

62. "The Common Sense Census: Media Use by Tweens and Teens, 2019," Common Sense Media, October 28, 2019, https://www.commonsensemedia.org/research/the-common-sense-census-media-use-by-tweens-and-teens-2019.

63. Monica Anderson and Jingjing Jiang, "Teens' Social Media Habits and Experiences," Pew Research Center, November 28, 2018, https://www.pewresearch.org/internet/2018/11/28/teens-social-media-habits-and-experiences/.

64. Anderson and Jiang, "Teens' Social Media Habits and Experiences."

65. Brian A. Primack, et al., "Social Media Use and Perceived Social Isolation Among Young Adults in the U.S.," American Journal of Preventive Medicine 53, no. 1 (2017): 1-8, https://doi.org/10.1016/j.amepre.2017.01.010.

66. Maeve Duggan, "Gaming and Gamers: The Role of Video Games in American Life," Pew Research Center, December 15, 2015, https://www.pewresearch.org/internet/2015/12/15/gaming-and-gamers/.

67. Monica Anderson and Jingjing Jiang, "Teens,

Social Media & Technology 2018," Pew Research Center, May 31, 2018, https://www.pewresearch.org/internet/2018/05/31/teens-social-media-technology-2018/.

68. Nicholas Kristof, "The Children of Pornhub," New York Times (New York City, NY), Dec. 4, 2020.

69. Pornhub, December 8, 2020, comment on Kristof, "The Children of Pornhub."

70. Kristof, "The Children of Pornhub."

71. Kristof, "The Children of Pornhub." (Ibid.)

72. Kristof, "The Children of Pornhub." (Ibid.)

73. Kristof, "The Children of Pornhub." (Ibid.)

74. Kristof, "The Children of Pornhub." (Ibid.)

75. Kristof, "The Children of Pornhub." (Ibid.)

76. Kristof, "The Children of Pornhub." (Ibid.)

77. Kristof, "The Children of Pornhub." (Ibid.)

78. "S.C.R. 9 Concurrent Resolution on the Public Health Crisis," Utah State Legislature, 2016, https://le.utah.gov/~2016/bills/static/scr009.html.

79. Mark Novicoff, "A Simple Law Is Doing the Impossible. It's Making the Online Porn Industry Retreat," Politico, August 8, 2023, https://www.politico.com/news/magazine/2023/08/08/age-law-online-porn-00110148.

80. Politico (2023), Pornhub's Response to State Legislation on Age Verification, retrieved from Politico.

81. A. Perry, "Billie Eilish Says Watching Porn Gave Her Nightmares and 'Destroyed' Her Brain," Guardian (Manchester, ENG), Dec. 14, 2021, https://www.theguardian.com/music/2021/dec/15/billie-eilish-says-watching-porn-gave-her-nightmares-and-destroyed-my-brain.

CHAPTER 5

82. Matt Walsh, "What is a Woman?" Daily Wirc, 2022, documentary, 1:35, https://www.dailywire.com/videos/what-is-a-woman.

83. Victor Salvo, "The Scientific-Humanitarian Committee," ed. Owen Keehnen, Legacy Project Chicago,

https://legacyprojectchicago.org/milestone/scientific-humanitarian-committee.

84. Matt Lebovic, "100 Years Ago, Germany's 'Einstein of Sex' Began the Gay Rights Movement," Times of Israel (Jerusalem, Israel), Nov. 11, 2019.

85. Lebovic, "100 Years Ago, Germany's 'Einstein of Sex...'"

86. Joanne Meyorwitz, How Sex Changed (Harvard University Press, 2002), 26.

87. Matt Walsh, What is a Woman?

88. James H. Jones, Alfred C. Kinsey: A Life (WW Norton, 2004), 622.

89. Theresa Gaffney, "'History Is Repeating Itself': The Story of the Nation's First Clinic for Gender-Affirming Surgery," STAT, October 3, 2022, https://www.statnews.com/2022/10/03/gender-affirming-surgery-hospitals-johns-hopkins/.

90. Meyerowitz, How Sex Changed.

91. Phil Gaetano, "David Reimer and John Money

Gender Reassignment Controversy: The John/Joan Case," ed. Claudia Nunez-Eddy, Embryo Project Encyclopedia, November 15, 2017, https://embryo.asu.edu/pages/david-reimer-and-john-money-gender-reassignment-controversy-johnjoan-case.

92. Phil Gaetano, "David Remer and John Money Gender Reassignment…"

93. Chloe Cole, "Transition Surgery Was the Biggest Mistake of My Life," PragerU, June 13, 2023, video, 10:05, https://www.prageru.com/video/chloe-cole-transition-surgery-was-the-biggest-mistake-of-my-life?utm_source=twitter&utm_medium=post&utm_campaign=sou.

94. "The Hippocratic Oath: First Do No Harm," Medical Aid, https://medicalaid.org/the-hippocratic-oath-first-do-no-harm/

95. "Lupron (Leuprolide): Uses & Side Effects," Cleveland Clinic, May 1, 2024, https://my.clevelandclinic.org/health/drugs/18166-leuprolide-injection.

96. "Puberty Blockers for Transgender and Gender-Diverse Youth," Mayo Clinic, June 14, 2023, https://www.mayoclinic.org/diseases-conditions/

gender-dysphoria/in-depth/pubertal-blockers/art-20459075.

97. Jane Robbins, "Why Puberty Blockers Are a Clear Danger to Children's Health," The Federalist, December 18, 2018, https://thefederalist.com/2018/12/14/puberty-blockers-clear-danger-childrens-health/.

98. Annelou L.C. de Vries, et al., "Puberty Suppression in Adolescents with Gender Identity Disorder: A Prospective Follow-Up Study," The Journal of Sexual Medicine 8, no. 8 (2011): 2276-2283.

99. Abigail Shrier, Irreversible Damage: The Transgender Craze Seducing Our Daughters (Regnery Publishing, 2020), PAGE NUMBER.

100. Jane Robbins, "The Cracks in the Edifice of Transgender Totalitarianism," Public Discourse, July 13, 2019, https://www.thepublicdiscourse.com/2019/07/54272/.

101. Rachel Levine, "Identity Denied: Trans in America," Nightline, July 14, 2023, video, 57, https://fb.watch/veqqY48mIy/.

102. Connell, Abigail, et al., "Mental Health and Sui-

cidality in Transgender Youth: A Systematic Review," Journal of the American Academy of Child and Adolescent Psychiatry 55, no. 8 (2016): 610-616, https://pubmed.ncbi.nlm.nih.gov/27343830/.

103. "Title IX of the Education Amendments of 1972, 20 U.S.C. § 1681," Civil Rights Division, August 6, 2015, https://www.justice.gov/crt/title-ix-education-amendments-1972#Sec.%201681.%20Sex.

104. "Protection of Women and Girls in Sports Act of 2023," GPO, April 10, 2023, https://www.congress.gov/118/crpt/hrpt35/CRPT-118hrpt35.pdf.

105. "Mother Speaks Out After 12-Year-Old Daughter Was Raped in School's Gender Fluid Bathroom," The Post Millennial, October 2021.

106. Luke Rosiak, "Loudoun Rapist Sentenced, Put on Sex Offender Registry for Life," Daily Wire, January 12, 2022, https://www.dailywire.com/news/breaking-loudoun-rapist-sentenced-put-on-sex-offender-registry-for-life.

107. Julianne McShane, "A Record Number of U.S. Adults Identify as LGBTQ. Gen Z Is Driving the Increase.," Washington Post (Washington, D.C.), Feb. 17, 2022.

CHAPTER 6

108. "Samuel Adams," Pondering Principles, https://ponderingprinciples.com/quotes/adams_s/.

109. Stephen Flick, "Benjamin Franklin and the Bible," Christian Heritage Fellowship, Inc., August 23, 2024, https://christianheritagefellowship.com/benjamin-franklin-and-the-bible/.

110. Grace Chen, "A History of Public Schools," Public School Review, March 7, 2022, https://www.publicschoolreview.com/blog/a-history-of-public-schools.

111. Chen, "A History of Public Schools."

112. "Critical Race Theory," Encyclopædia Britannica, September 16, 2024, https://www.britannica.com/topic/critical-race-theory.

113. James Lindsay and Helen Pluckrose, Cynical Theories: How Activist Scholarship Made Everything about Race, Gender, and Identity—and Why This Harms Everybody (Pitchstone Publishing, 2020), PAGE NUMBER.

114. Tom Pappert, "Sources Confirm Docs Leaked by Crowder Are Authentic Covenant Killer Writings,

MNPD Investigating," Tennessee Star (Franklin, TN), Nov. 6, 2023, https://tennesseestar.com/justice/sources-confirm-docs-leaked-by-crowder-are-authentic-covenant-killer-writings-mnpd-investigating/tpappert/2023/11/06/.

115. "Marjorie Taylor Greene Claims Shooter Manifestos Should Be Public," News Outlet.

116. James Lindsay, "The Proximate Ideological Origins of Critical Race Theory," YouTube, February 23, 2022, video, 1:16:25, https://www.youtube.com/watch?v=OQ7vBukc9gM.

117. Peggy McIntosh, "White Privilege: Unpacking the Invisible Knapsack," Wellesley Centers for Women, 1989, https://www.wcwonline.org/Fact-Sheets-Briefs/white-privilege-unpacking-the-invisible-knapsack-2.

118. "Critical Race Theory and Its Origins," UCLA School of Public Affairs, https://ncwsroom.ucla.edu/stories/20-years-critical-race-studies-ucla-law

119. "Critical Race Theory and Its Origins,"... (Ibid.)

120. Voddie Baucham, Fault Lines: The Social Justice Movement and Evangelicalism's Looming Catastro-

phe (Salem Books, 2021), PAGE NUMBER.

121. Antonio Gramsci, Prison Notebooks, ed. Joseph A. Buttigieg (Columbia University Press, 1992-2007).

122. "The History of Prayer Being Removed from Schools," Great American Pure Flix, October 13, 2017, https://www.pureflix.com/insider/the-history-of-prayer-being-removed-from-schools.

123. "The History of Prayer…," Great American Pure Flix.

124. "The History of Prayer…," Great American Pure Flix.

125. "Adolescent Family Life Act," American Civil Liberties Union, accessed August 20, 2024, https://www.laaclu.org/en/news/inside-one-governors-crusade-tear-down-wall-between-church-and-state.

126. "Abstinence and Abstinence-Only Education," National Library of Medicine, April 27, 2018, https://www.ncbi.nlm.nih.gov/pmc/articles/PMC5913747/.

127. "History of Sex Education in the U.S.," Planned Parenthood, November 2016, https://cdn.plannedparenthood.org/uploads/filer_public/da/67/da67fd5d-631d-438a-85e8-a446d90fd1e3/20170209_sexed_

d04_1.pdf.

128. "History of Sex Education...," Planned Parenthood.

129. Hope Sloop, "Undercover Video Reveals Dean of Elite Chicago School Bragging About Handing Out Dildos, Butt Plugs, and Lube to Students as Young as 14..." Daily Mail Online, December 8, 2022, https://www.dailymail.co.uk/news/article-11517503/Dean-Chicago-school-says-students-shown-dildos-butt-plugs-teaching-queer-sex.html.

130. "U.S. Department of Education's 2024 Title IX Final Rule Overview," U.S. Department of Education, July 31, 2024, https://www.ed.gov/sites/ed/files/about/offices/list/ocr/docs/t9-final-rule-factsheet.pdf.

131. Clay Olsen, "A Love Letter from the Co-Founder and President of Fight the New Drug," Fight the New Drug, November 1, 2021, https://fightthenewdrug.org/love-letter-clay-olsen-ceo-fight-the-new-drug/.

132. "Founders Online: Thomas Jefferson to Joseph C. Cabell, 2 February 1816," National Archives and Records Administration, accessed August 20, 2024, https://founders.archives.gov/documents/Jeffer-

son/03-09-02-0286.

133. Linda Greenhouse, "Parents Upheld on Committing Minor Children," New York Times (New York City, NY), Jun. 21, 1979, https://www.nytimes.com/1979/06/21/archives/parents-upheld-on-committing-minor-children-high-court-backs-states.html.

134. Lindsay Kornick, "Karine Jean-Pierre Slams Bans on Trans Treatment for Minors: 'These Are Our Kids, They Belong to All of Us,'" Fox News, May 17, 2023, https://www.foxnews.com/media/karine-jean-pierre-slams-bans-trans-treatment-minors-kids-belong-us.

135. "California Cradle-to-Career Data System," C2C, November 29, 2023, https://c2c.ca.gov/.

136. William J. Bennett, "Obama's 'The Life of Julia' Is the Wrong Vision for America," CNN online, May 9, 2012, https://www.cnn.com/2012/05/09/opinion/bennett-obama-campaign/index.html.

137. Bennett, "Obama's 'The Life of Julia...'"

138. "News Conference—I'm Here to Help," The Ronald Reagan Presidential Foundation & Institute,

August 12, 1986, https://www.reaganfoundation.org/ronald-reagan/reagan-quotes-speeches/news-conference-1/.

139. "Spurious Quotations," George Washington's Mount Vernon, https://www.mountvernon.org/library/digitalhistory/digital-encyclopedia/article/spurious-quotations/.

140. Penny Nance, "My Son's Freshman Orientation at Virginia Tech Was Full of Leftist Propaganda," The Federalist, August 14, 2019, https://thefederalist.com/2019/08/14/sons-freshman-orientation-virginia-tech-full-leftist-propaganda/.

141. Georgia Purdom, "Harvard: No Longer 'Truth for Christ and the Church,'" Answers in Genesis, October 11, 2011, https://answersingenesis.org/blogs/georgia-purdom/2011/10/11/harvard-no-longer-truth-for-christ-and-the-church/.

142. "Abolish the White Race," Harvard Magazine, September–October 2002, https://www.harvardmagazine.com/2002/09/abolish-the-white-race.html.

143. "Quote by H.L. Mencken," Liberty Tree, accessed August 27, 2024, http://libertytree.ca/quotes/H..L..

Mencken.Quote.57A5.

Chapter 7

144. Claudia Nunez-Eddy, "The Malthusian League (1877–1927)," Embryo Project Encyclopedia, April 27, 2017, https://embryo.asu.edu/pages/malthusian-league-1877-1927.

145. Nunez-Eddy, "The Malthusian League…"

146. Francis Galton, "Eugenics: Its Definition, Scope and Aims," galton.org, July 1904, https://galton.org/essays/1900-1911/galton-1904-am-journ-soc-eugenics-scope-aims.htm.

147. Galton, "Eugenics: Its Definition…"

148. Brian Clowes, "The Strange World of Margaret Sanger's Birth Control Review," Human Life International, April 18, 2017, https://www.hli.org/resources/sangers-birth-control-review-part-i/.

149. "Margaret Sanger," Encyclopædia Britannica, accessed August 27, 2024, https://www.britannica.com/explore/100women/profiles/margaret-sanger.

150. "History of Planned Parenthood," Planned Parenthood, accessed August 27, 2024, https://www.plannedparenthood.org/about-us/who-we-are/our-history.

151. Clowes, "The Strange World of Margaret Sanger…"

152. Raymond Fosdick, "Letter to John D. Rockefeller, Jr., June 13, 1924," Rockefeller Archive Center (RAC), Rockefeller Family Boards, RG III 2 K, box 1, folder 1.

153. Donald T. Critchlow, (1995). "Birth Control, Population Control, and Family Planning: An Overview," Journal of Policy History 6, no. 1 (1995): 1-21.

154. "Planned Parenthood," Rockefeller Brothers Fund, 1942, https://www.rbf.org/about/our-history/timeline/planned-parenthood.

155. "The Link Between Contraceptive Pills and Depression," Neuroscience News, June 13, 2023, https://neurosciencenews.com/depression-contraceptive-pills-23451/.

156. "History of Planned Parenthood," Planned Parenthood.

157. "About," National Organization for Women, accessed August 27, 2024, https://now.org/about/.

158. "About," National Organization for Women.

159. Sepehr Abdi-Moradi, "Betty Friedan (1921–2006)," Embryo Project Encyclopedia, June 15, 2017, https://embryo.asu.edu/pages/betty-friedan-1921-2006.

160. "History of Planned Parenthood," Planned Parenthood.

161. "Bush Reverses Abortion Aid," Washington Post (Washington, D.C.), Jan. 23, 2001, https://www.washingtonpost.com/archive/politics/2001/01/23/bush-reverses-abortion-aid/.

162. "History of Planned Parenthood," Planned Parenthood.

163. Merriam-Webster: America's Most Trusted Dictionary (Merriam-Webster), s.v. "Medical," https://www.merriam-webster.com/dictionary/medical.

164. "Comprehensive Abortion Care," National Library of Medicine, accessed August 27, 2024, https://www.ncbi.nlm.nih.gov/books/NBK305158/.

165. "The Abortion Pill (RU-486)," Illinois Right to Life, accessed August 27, 2024, https://illinoisrighttolife.org/abortion-pill-ru-486/.

166. "The Abortion Pill (RU-486)," Illinois Right to Life.

167. "The Abortion Pill (RU-486)," Illinois Right to Life. (Ibid.)

168. "The Abortion Pill (RU-486)," Illinois Right to Life. (Ibid.)

169. "Risk Factors for Legal Induced Abortion," National Library of Medicine, accessed August 27, 2024, https://pubmed.ncbi.nlm.nih.gov/15051566/.

170. "D&E Abortion Procedure," Abortion Procedures, https://www.abortionprocedures.com/.

171. "What Can I Expect After an In-Clinic Abortion?" Planned Parenthood, accessed August 27, 2024, https://www.plannedparenthood.org/learn/abortion/in-clinic-abortion-procedures/what-can-i-expect-after-having-an-in-clinic-abortion.

172. "Abortion and Mental Health: A Systematic Review of the Literature," British Journal of Psychiatry 199, no. 3 (2011): 180-186, https://www.cambridge.org/core/journals/the-british-journal-of-psychiatry/article/abortion-and-mental-health-quantitative-synthesis-and-analysis-of-research-published-19952009/E8D556AAE1C1D2F0F8B060B28BEE6C3D.

173. "How Does Abortion Affect Mental Health? Does It Have an Impact?" Laguna Treatment Hospital, June 13, 2024, https://lagunatreatment.com/support-for-women/mental-health-abortion/.

174. "For Men," Post Abortion Treatment and Healing, https://www.healingafterabortion.org/for-men.html.

175. Joan Boydell, "A Study of Suffering After Abortion," Care-Net, February 19, 2018, https://www.care-net.org/center-insights-blog/a-study-of-suffering-after-abortion.

176. Jerome LeJeune, "Testimony Before the U.S. Senate Judiciary Subcommittee on Constitutional Rights," U.S. Senate, 1981, https://www.senate.gov.

177. Alfred M. Bongioanni, "Testimony before the U.S. Senate Judiciary Subcommittee on Constitutional Rights," U.S. Senate, 1981, https://www.senate.gov.

178. Bernard Nathanson, The Hand of God: A Journey from Death to Life by the Creator of the Silent Scream (Regnery Publishing, 1996), PAGE NUMBER.

179. "Who We Are," Planned Parenthood, accessed August 27, 2024, https://www.plannedparenthood.org/about-us/who-we-are.

Chapter 8

180. James Wilson, Works of James Wilson, ed. Robert Green McCloskey, vol. 1 (Harvard University Press, 1967).

181. Wilson, Works of James Wilson, PAGE NUMBER.

182. "Modern Parenthood: Roles of Moms and Dads Converge as They Balance Work and Family," Pew Research Center, March 14, 2013, https://www.pewresearch.org/social-trends/2013/03/14/modern-parenthood-roles-of-moms-and-dads-converge-as-they-bal-

ance-work-and-family/.

183. "The Link Between Family Structure and Child Well-Being," Pew Research Center, November 20, 2014, https://www.pewresearch.org/short-reads/2019/12/12/u-s-children-more-likely-than-children-in-other-countries-to-live-with-just-one-parent/.

184. "The Link Between Family Structure and Criminal Behavior," Office of National Drug Control Policy, 2003, https://www.whitehouse.gov/ondcp/.

185. James Wilson, Lectures on Law, ed. Robert Green McCloskey, vol. 2 (Harvard University Press, 1967), PAGE NUMBER.

186. Robert Owen, A New View of Society and Other Writings, ed. Richard L. Bushman (Penguin Classics, 1991), PAGE NUMBER.

187. Friedrich Engels, The Origin of the Family, Private Property and the State, ed. Eleanor Burke Leacock (International Publishers, 1972), PAGE NUMBER.

188. Betty Friedan, The Feminine Mystique (W. W.

Norton & Company, 1963), PAGE NUMBER.

190. Germaine Greer, The Female Eunuch (Harper & Row, 1970), PAGE NUMBER.

191. "Health, United States, 2019," Centers for Disease Control and Prevention, 2020, https://www.cdc.gov/nchs/data/hus/hus19-508.pdf.

192. D'Vera Cohn, "Love and Marriage," Pew Research Center, February 13, 2013, https://www.pewresearch.org/social-trends/2013/02/13/love-and-marriage/

193. Engels, The Origin of the Family, Private Property and the State, PAGE NUMBER.

194. Patrick Henry, Letters of Patrick Henry, ed. William Wirt (John C. Winston Company, 1913).

195. "Election Polls and Trends," Gallup, 2020, https://news.gallup.com.

196. Leon Trotsky, "Letter to Vladimir Lenin," 1911, https://www.marxists.org/archive/trotsky/works/.

197. "The Impact of Marriage on Economic Stability," Pew Research Center, 2020, https://www.pewresearch.org.

198. "The Balance of Work and Family Life," Pew Research Center, 2021, https://www.pewresearch.org.

199. "Strong Families as Seedbeds for Virtues," Institute for Family Studies, 2023, https://ifstudies.org.

200. "Strong Families as Seedbeds for Virtues," Institute for Family Studies.

201. "Strong Families as Seedbeds for Virtues," Institute for Family Studies.

202. "Strong Families and Economic Well-Being," Institute for Family Studies, 2023, https://ifstudies.org.

203. Brad Wilcox and Robert I. Lerman, "For Richer, for Poorer: How Family Structures Economic Success in America," American Enterprise Institute - AEI, October 8, 2014, https://www.aei.org/research-products/report/for-richer-for-poorer-how-family-structures-economic-success-in-america/.

Chapter 9

204. Thomas Jefferson, Notes on the State of Virginia, ed. William Peden (University of North Carolina Press, 1955), PAGE NUMBER.

205. James Madison, Memorial and Remonstrance Against Religious Assessments, 1785, ed. Robert A. Rutland (University of Virginia Press, 1986), PAGE NUMBER.

206. Thomas Jefferson, The Papers of Thomas Jefferson, ed. Julian P. Boyd, vol. 10 (Princeton University Press, 1953), PAGE NUMBER.

207. G.K. Chesterton, Heretics, ed. E. B. White (Image Books, 2001), PAGE NUMBER.

208. "Marxism and the United States: The Challenge of the New Marxism," The Heritage Foundation, 2024, https://www.heritage.org.

209. James Madison, "Federalist No. 55," in The Federalist Papers, ed. Clinton Rossiter (New American Library, 1961), 349-357.

210. Alexis de Tocqueville, Democracy in America, eds. Harvey C. Mansfield and Delba Winthrop, trans. George Lawrence (University of Chicago Press, 2000), 505.

211. Ronald Reagan, "Inaugural Address," in The Papers of Ronald Reagan: The California Years, eds. Douglas Brinkley and James R. Halstead, vol. 1 (University of Virginia Press, 2006), 95–100.

212. John Adams, The Quotable John Adams, ed. Michael J. O'Brien (Yale University Press, 2007), 123.

213. Benjamin Franklin, The Founding Fathers on the Constitution, ed. Bruce A. Ragsdale (Oxford University Press, 2000), 45.

CliffNotes
Chapter-by-Chapter

CHAPTER 1:
THE FOUNDING OF THE
AMERICAN NATION

1. The Birth of a Nation: Independence Declared. The importance of *The Declaration of Independence* and the American colonies' desire for religious freedom.

2. The Fight for Religious Freedom: Why It Mattered. How religious persecution in England and Europe led to the Pilgrims' quest for freedom.

3. Bradford's Brave Choice: The Power of Faith at Age 16. How William Bradford's inspiring decision to leave his family and follow his faith shaped his future as a leader.

4. Escape to Freedom: The Pilgrims' Dangerous Journey. The challenges and dangers faced by the Pilgrims as they fled to Holland for religious freedom.

5. Sailing to a New Life: The Mayflower's Journey. How the stormy 66-day voyage to America and the Pilgrims' drafting of the *Mayflower Compact* established their self-governance.

6. The *Mayflower Compact*: Building a Government on Faith. How the *Mayflower Compact* laid the groundwork for America's founding principles and self-rule.

7. Self-Government: The Pilgrims' Vision for a Free Society. How self-governance became a core value of American liberty.

8. Lessons from England: Overcoming Tyranny. How Pilgrims learned the value of freedom from England's oppressive rule and translated that into the foundation of America.

9. A Nation of Freedom: The Revolutionary War and Independence. How in 1776 the creation of a new nation built on God-inspired ideas of freedom and independence.

10. What Makes America Exceptional? How the six principles of American Exceptionalism make the country stand out.

11. From Freedom to Prosperity: Why America Thrives. How the reasons why America became a

prosperous and free nation became admired by many around the world.

12. America's Youth: What Does Freedom Mean to You? A reflection on why younger generations should feel proud of America's legacy of freedom and opportunity.

13. God's Role in America's Success: Blessings and Challenges. How America's acknowledgment of God's role in its foundation has led to its success and the challenges of staying on the right path.

14. Modern Challenges: Is America Still Honoring God? Examining current policies and whether they align with Biblical principles, and what this means for America's future.

15. Choosing Leaders with Values: Why It Matters. The importance of electing morally strong, Biblically-literate leaders to guide the nation.

16. America's Imperfect Path: Learning from History. A recognition that while America isn't perfect, its foundation on faith and freedom has led it to greatness.

17. What Does "Separation of Church and State" Really Mean? Understanding the basics and debunking the confusion around Thomas Jefferson's famous statement.

18. Bad Calls: How Politics Misuses "Separation of Church and State." The ways the government and media misuse this term to target Christian values.

19. The Dark Side of Government-Sponsored Religion. How child sacrifice and hedonism are being imposed on Americans today.

20. Lessons from History: When the Church and State Collide. Examples from Rome and England where state-controlled religion led to tyranny.

21. Meet Reverend Thomas Hooker: A Hero for Religious Freedom. The story of a Puritan leader who protected the Church from government interference.

22. Why the Pilgrims Fled: Escaping Forced Religion. How early settlers sought freedom from government-imposed faith.

23. Thomas Jefferson's "Wall": Protecting the Church, Not Removing God. Jefferson's real intent behind the "Wall of Separation" and why it matters.

24. Charles Galloway: Why Christianity Should Still Shape Our Laws. How a Methodist bishop explained the role of faith in America's government.

25. America's Foundation: Built on Faith and Freedom. How God and His laws shaped the greatness of America.

26. Read This Every Day: *The Founders' Bible.* Why the Bible, infused with American history, is key to understanding our nation's roots.

CHAPTER 2
SILENCED AND CENSORED

1. Silenced and Censored: The Fight for Religious Freedom Today. How the government is stripping away the right to speak and worship freely.

2. Alexis de Tocqueville's America: Freedom and Faith United. The powerful insights of a French philosopher on America's unique blend of freedom and religion.

3. Roger Williams and Rhode Island: Pioneering Religious Freedom. How one of the first American colonies led the way in protecting religious rights.

4. The First Amendment: America's Promise of Religious Freedom. Understanding the most important constitutional protection for freedom of worship.

5. Eric Metaxas on What We've Forgotten About Religious Freedom. A bestselling author's take on how modern America misunderstands its history.

6. The Pilgrims' Escape: From Persecution to True Freedom. Why the Pilgrims' fight for religious freedom still matters today.

7. No Religion Imposed, But Freedom to Choose. How the First Amendment protects religious expression without forcing beliefs.

8. The Danger of Losing Our Right to Speak Freely. Why free speech and religious freedom are essential for America's success.

9. A Society Without God Can't Survive. Why faith is critical to the survival and growth of any nation, especially America.

10. The 2020 PLANdemic: Churches Closed, Bars Open. How the pandemic restrictions unfairly targeted places of worship while allowing other establishments to stay open.

11. Standing Up to Government Overreach: Churches Fight Back. Chicago churches face fines and restrictions, and the battle for religious freedom intensifies.

12. Masking Love or Misinformation? Examining the call to "love your neighbor" by wearing masks, and why some Christians pushed back against this message.

13. Masks: Freedom vs. Fear. Why masks became a symbol of control for some, and the debate over health, freedom, and individual choice.

14. Vaccines and Religious Exemptions: A Fight for Freedom. The struggle over forced vaccinations and religious rights in the workplace.

15. Losing Jobs Over Principles: Americans' Livelihoods at Risk. How people lost careers and licenses for standing up against vaccine mandates.

16. Spiritual Warfare in a Time of Crisis. Viewing the pandemic as more than a health crisis—a spiritual battle over community and connection.

17. Winning for Religious Freedom: The Case of Masterpiece Cakeshop. How a baker stood up for his First Amendment rights and won.

18. Web Designers and Wedding Websites: A Win for Free Speech. The 303 Creative case and the victory for religious freedom in the digital age.

19. What's ESG and Why Should We Care? Explaining the dangers of ESG scores and how they affect businesses and religious freedom.

20. Fighting Back Against ESG: Boycotts and Small Businesses. How Americans can push back against corporate control by supporting local and small businesses.

21. Government-Sponsored Beliefs: Abortion and Critical Race Theory. How the government is pushing controversial ideologies through public funding and education.

22. The Backpack Kid and the Gadsden Flag. The story of Jaiden and his stand for free speech at school.

23. Silent Prayer, Loud Consequences: Arrested for Believing. How silently praying outside an abortion clinic led to an arrest—and what it means for religious freedom.

24. Pro-Life Heroes or Criminals? The Joan Bell Case. How a 74-year-old woman was imprisoned for defending the unborn in America.

25. Fairness in Sports? Women are Silenced and Men Compete. The story of William Thomas (Lia) and the fight for fairness in women's sports.

26. President Obama's Impact on Religious Freedom. Explores policies during Obama's administration that affected religious liberties, particularly focusing on the Department of Health and Human Services' contraception rule.

27. The January 6th Controversy: What Really Happened? Details events surrounding January 6, 2021, and questions the media's portrayal of the protest as an insurrection.

28. Inside Job or Peaceful Protest? Investigates claims of government involvement in the January 6 protest and challenges the narrative of an insurrection.

29. What the Media Doesn't Want You to Know About January 6. Why certain footage and information were hidden and how big tech, media, and politics may be manipulating public perception.

30. BLM Riots vs. January 6: A Double Standard? Compares the reaction to the 2020 BLM protests and riots with the response to January 6, questioning the focus on the Capitol incident.

31. The FBI, Big Tech, and the 2020 Election. Examines the role of the FBI and Silicon Valley in censoring conservative voices leading up to the 2020 election.

32. My Family's Story: Persecution for Supporting Trump. A personal story about how political and religious beliefs led to accusations of racism and homophobia within a youth baseball league.

33. What is Marxism, and Why Should You Care? Defines Marxism and explains how it relates to the separation of society into categories of oppressed and oppressors.

34. The Slow Process of Brainwashing: What Yuri Bezmenov Warned Us About. A look at Yuri Bezmenov's warnings about ideological subversion and how it's shaping today's society.

35. Why Religious Liberty is at Risk in America. A call to action for defending religious and personal freedoms, explaining the stakes for American citizens.

CHAPTER 3:
SHALL NOT BE INFRINGED

1. What Does the Second Amendment Really Mean? Introduces the Second Amendment and its original intent.

2. From Ancient Warriors to American Freedom Fighters. Traces the history of the right to bear arms, from ancient Rome to the founding of the U.S.

3. Guns: A Natural Right or a Privilege? Explains how the right to bear arms is considered a natural law, not a government gift.

4. Why the Second Amendment Exists. Discusses the Second Amendment's purpose—protection from a tyrannical government, not just target practice.

5. How Politicians are Threatening Our Gun Rights. Highlights current challenges to gun rights, including politicians using safety as a reason to restrict guns.

6. The Truth About Gun-Free Zones. Explores how gun-free zones may be making things worse by attracting criminals.

7. The Nashville School Shooting: What Aren't They Telling Us? Investigates why certain shooter manifestos, like Audrey Hale's in Nashville, are kept from the public.

8. Who Profits from Gun Control? A look at who benefits from stricter gun laws—hint, it's not law-abiding citizens.

9. How Gun Control Can Lead to More Control. Examines historical examples where gun control led to dictatorships, such as in Stalin's and Mao's regimes.

10. What's Really Behind Red Flag Laws? A critical look at red flag laws and how they could be used to unfairly strip people of their rights.

11. Social Media and Guns: Watch What You Post! Warns about laws that could deny gun permits based on what people post on social media.

12. Could Social Credit Scores Come to America? Explains how China's social credit system might be creeping into America's gun laws.

CHAPTER 4:
THE DIGITAL AGE

1. The Power of Words: How Media Shapes Society. Explore how the media influences societal perceptions and behaviors, especially in matters of race, gender, and culture.

2. Klaus Schwab and the Future of Technology. Introduction to key figures like Klaus Schwab and the impact of global organizations on technological developments.

3. Tech's Blessing and Curse: Connecting the World, Disrupting Lives. Discuss the dual nature of technology, with its potential to connect people globally while also causing personal disconnection.

4. The Social Media Trap: The Price of Instant Connection. A breakdown of how social media has led to disconnection from reality, rising mental health issues, and decreased face-to-face interactions.

5. Teens and Tech: Nine Hours a Day Online. Focus on Generation Z's excessive media consumption and how it affects their social lives and mental health.

6. Loneliness in a Hyper-Connected World. Highlight how constant social media use actually increases feelings of loneliness and isolation.

7. Predators on the Web: The Hidden Dangers of Social Media. A look at the alarming reality of online predators targeting children and teens, especially during the COVID-19 pandemic.

8. The Omegle Story: How an App Put Children at Risk. Delve into the history of the Omegle app and its closure due to exploitation, highlighting the ongoing issue of online safety.

9. The Rise of Fake Profiles: How Predators Lure Teens. Explain how predators use fake accounts on social media platforms to manipulate and exploit young users.

10. The Dangers of Social Media: A Must-Watch Experiment. Introduction to parents of the popular video by Coby Persin, showing how easily teens can be tricked by online predators.

11. Pornography and Its Impact on Young Minds. Explore the devastating effects of early exposure to pornography, including its role in the larger issue of sex trafficking.

12. Pornhub Exposed: The Dark Side of the Porn Industry. A deep dive into the exposés revealing Pornhub's exploitation of children and the call for its shutdown.

13. Can Pornhub Ever Be Stopped? Discuss the ongoing fight to shut down porn platforms profiting from exploitation, and the challenges ahead.

14. Even Insiders Know: Porn Destroys Lives. Reveal shocking admissions from Pornhub executives about the harmful, addictive nature of pornography.

15. Protecting Our Future: What Can We Do? Offer practical advice on how parents and society can fight against the harmful influence of pornography and social media.

16. Big Tech: Who's Watching Out for Us? Discusses how companies like Netflix, Google, and Apple aren't doing enough to protect children from online dangers.

17. Where Are the Rules? Explores why there are no laws stopping online predators and how Big Tech can make changes but chooses not to.

18. The Hidden Agenda Behind Big Tech. Explains how some Big Tech founders are connected to groups like the World Economic Forum and how this relates to a global power agenda.

19. Big Tech and Politics: Who's Really in Charge? Reveals the connections between Big Tech and politicians and how this influences our lives.

20. You Are Your Child's Best Defender. Empowers parents to take control of their children's safety rather than relying on the state or Big Tech.

21. Keeping an Eye on What Your Kids Are Learning. Encourages parents to be aware of what's being taught in schools, even at the kindergarten level.

22. Raising Strong Kids in a Weak World. Talks about teaching children values, limiting their online access, and protecting their innocence.

23. The Truth About the Sex Industry. Breaks down misconceptions about sexual liberation, especially the exploitation of women and children.

24. Women Deserve Better: The Real Cost of "Empowerment." Focuses on how women and young girls are harmed by the commercial sex industry, despite claims of empowerment.

25. Redefining Manliness in a Confused World. Calls for a return to Biblical manhood to counter society's moral decline.

CHAPTER FIVE:
THE POISON OF
GENDER IDEOLOGY

1. God's Blueprint: Man and Woman. Introduces the Biblical foundation of gender as created by God.

2. How Gender Ideology Changed Everything. Explores the impact of gender ideology on modern culture, from advertisements to education.

3. Matt Walsh's Eye-Opening Journey: *What is a Woman?* Discusses the documentary *What is a Woman?* and its exposure of the confusion surrounding gender.

4. The Roots of Gender Ideology: Magnus Hirschfeld. Examines how the work of Magnus Hirschfeld laid the groundwork for today's gender discussions.

5. Germany's "Einstein of Sex" and the Third Gender Idea. Focuses on Hirschfeld's concept of a "third sex" and his role in shaping LGBTQ rights.

6. The Rise of Gender Medicine: Harry Benjamin. Details how Harry Benjamin contributed to the belief that gender could be changed through medical procedures.

7. Alfred Kinsey's Dangerous Agenda. Highlights Alfred Kinsey's influence on society's views of sexuality, including his disturbing ideas about children.

8. John Money's Dark Legacy. Introduces John Money and his role in separating gender from sex and advocating for gender reassignment surgeries.

9. The Tragic Story of the Reimer Twins. Tells the heartbreaking story of the Reimer twins and the devastating effects of John Money's theories.

10. The Cost of Lies: How Gender Ideology Hurts Lives. Focuses on the human cost of gender ideology, including confusion, pain, and loss of life, as seen in the case of David Reimer.

11. A Family's Unexpected Journey. Introduction to the transgender issue from a personal perspective, following the tragic accident that changed the author's family forever.

12. Inside the Medical System: A Closer Look. The experience of seeing how gender ideology was being pushed in medical facilities, with constant exposure to pronoun pins and rainbow imagery.

13. Meeting the Doctors: Confusion at the Clinic. A firsthand encounter with a resident doctor displaying pronoun pins and the troubling realization of their influence on children's health.

14. When Medical Care Becomes a Trend. A reflection on how society and medicine seem to be elevating confused individuals into authority positions and questioning the safety of their influence.

15. From a Personal Struggle to a Public Stand. Realizing the scale of the issue, the author describes their decision to step up, pray, and act against what was happening to minors.

16. Teens Against Gender Mutilation: The First Rally. The story of how a pro-life rally turned into the first Teens Against Gender Mutilation rally and what surprised the author most during the promotion.

17. Doubters and Critics: Facing Opposition. Encountering disbelief and criticism, including a radio host who called the author "brainwashed" for speaking

out on these issues.

18. The Church's Silence: Disappointment in Christian Leaders. A reflection on how local churches and Christian leaders were too afraid to support the rally or speak up about the dangers of gender ideology.

19. What the Bible Says: A Spiritual Perspective. A discussion on why the issue of transgenderism is more than political—it's a spiritual attack on the body, created in God's image.

20. Standing for Truth in a Confused World. An appeal to pastors and Christians to speak out boldly, teaching the truth about gender and God's design, even if it's controversial.

21. The Media's Spin: Dealing with Backlash. Describing how the media twisted the event into an "anti-trans" rally and the pushback received from various counter-protests.

22. Chloe Cole's Story: A Heartbreaking Journey. Introducing Chloe Cole, an eighteen-year-old detransitioner, and sharing her devastating experiences with hormone therapy and surgery.

23. The Real Cost of Transitioning. The aftermath of Chloe Cole's transition, including her regret and the irreversible damage done to her body and future.

24. A Call to Protect the Innocent. Closing with the rally's purpose: to protect children from harmful surgeries and hormone treatments, while standing for truth and love.

25. The Doctor's Promise: "Do No Harm!" An introduction to the Hippocratic Oath and its core principle of not harming patients.

26. A Strange Request: Cutting Off My Arm? An analogy exploring the idea of how no sane doctor would amputate a healthy limb, tying it to the topic of gender surgeries.

27. Breaking the Oath: Doctors and Gender Surgeries. Examining how some doctors are abandoning their commitment to "Do no harm" by encouraging gender-altering treatments for children.

28. Puberty Blockers: The Dangerous Pause. A deep dive into Lupron, its history, and the harmful effects it has on children under the guise of pausing puberty.

29. Side Effects: When Health Is Shattered. Sharing the severe and long-term consequences of puberty blockers like Lupron, from joint pain to suicidal thoughts.

30. Cross-Sex Hormones: The Point of No Return. Highlighting the irreversible damage caused by cross-sex hormones, particularly infertility and arrested sexual development.

31. What Happens If You Change Your Mind? Exploring the lasting physical changes and hardships faced by those who regret their transition.

32. The Gruesome Reality of "Bottom Surgery." A candid look at the horrifying details and risks of sex reassignment surgeries, from mutilation to painful lifelong aftercare.

33. Where Do We Draw the Line? Asking the tough questions about how far society will go, discussing the slippery slope of normalizing extreme behaviors.

34. The Ripple Effect of Moral Shifts. Tracing the cultural changes from the acceptance of sex outside of marriage to the current debates over child gender surgeries.

35. Ignoring the Warning Signs: Society's Dangerous Path. Pointing out the dangers of abandoning moral standards, with the transgender movement leading the charge.

36. The Truth Behind Transgender Suicide Risks. Addressing the troubling statistics of high suicide rates among transgender individuals despite gender-affirming care.

37. When Science and Faith Collide. Highlighting the conflict between science, biblical teachings, and the growing cultural acceptance of gender ideology.

38. What Title IX Was Supposed to Do. Explaining Title IX and its original goal to provide equal opportunities for girls in sports and education.

39. Back to Square One: Fighting for Girls' Rights Again. How gender ideology is reversing years of progress by allowing men into women's sports and safe spaces.

40. A Common-Sense Bill Rejected. The surprising rejection of the Protection of Women and Girls in Sports Act of 2023 by Democrats in Congress.

41. The Cost of Inclusion: My Locker Room Experience. A personal story of discomfort and invasion of privacy at a local swimming pool.

42. Whose Rights Matter More? The conflict between cross-dressing men's rights and the privacy and safety of women in bathrooms and locker rooms.

43. Kylee Alons: Speaking Out for Fair Play. The story of a decorated swimmer forced to compete against a male athlete and her decision to change in a janitor's closet.

44. Payton McNabb: Injured by Unfair Competition. How a male volleyball player's spike left a female player with long-lasting injuries, highlighting the physical dangers of unfair competition.

45. A Shocking Reality: Girls at Risk. Real-life examples of how gender ideology policies have led to assaults and rapes in schools.

46. The Case of ASK Academy. A heartbreaking story of a young girl who was raped in a gender-neutral bathroom and the devastating impact on her life.

47. Standing Up Against the Lies. How a father's outcry after his daughter was assaulted in a gender-neutral bathroom led to his arrest and the exposure of school corruption.

48. Danger in the Ring: When Females Face Males in Sports. A female boxer's decision to quit a fight after 46 seconds to avoid serious injury from a male opponent.

49. The Flimsy Arguments: Intersex and Acceptance. Debunking the common arguments about intersex conditions and the push for acceptance of harmful ideolo-

gies.

50. The Rainbow Cult: A Religious Movement? Comparing the LGBTQ movement to a religious cult that demands worship of sin and sexual immorality.

51. The Real Battle: Holiness and Choices. Addressing the deeper issue of morality and choices in the context of the LGBTQ movement versus traditional values.

52. Red Herrings and Distractions. Calling out the logical fallacies used to deflect from the real issues at stake in the debate over gender and sports.

53. The Simple Truth: Only Two Genders. Clarifying the belief that gender is unchangeable and assigned by God at conception.

54. Why Society Needs Common Sense. Exploring the idea that without traditional gender roles and family structures, society and civilization would collapse.

55. The Bible Speaks: Gender Roles Matter. A look at biblical teachings on men and women's roles and how dressing as the opposite gender is viewed as an abomination.

56. Counseling Can Only Go So Far. Addressing the limitations of therapy and medical interventions for those struggling with gender identity, and emphasizing the need for spiritual truth.

57. True Freedom Comes Through Christ. Highlighting the belief that true freedom and healing can only be found in the Bible and through a relationship with Jesus Christ.

58. Generation Z: The Struggle is Real. Discussing the rise in depression and anxiety among Gen Z and linking it to the growing embrace of LGBTQ identities and anti-God narratives.

59. The Dangerous Cocktail of Social Media and Gender Fluidity. Examining how social media and gender ideology are contributing to a mental health crisis among young people.

CHAPTER 6:
EDUCATION

1. Samuel Adams' Call: Why Education Matters. Exploring Samuel Adams' belief in the importance of educating young boys and girls with Christian values for a strong nation.

2. How Thomas Jefferson Shaped Public Education. A look at Thomas Jefferson's vision for a public educational system and how it set the stage for modern schooling.

3. From Biblical Principles to Schools for All. How early American education was based on teaching morality through the Bible and the evolution to education for

all students.

4. The Birth of Modern Schooling: Horace Mann's Impact. Horace Mann's contributions to shaping American education, from grading systems to training teachers.

5. Segregation to Integration: *Brown v. Board of Education*. Understanding the journey from racial segregation in schools to the landmark Supreme Court decision that ended it.

6. The Rise of Critical Race Theory (CRT). Introducing Critical Race Theory and how it claims that laws and institutions are inherently racist, challenging students to see society through the lens of oppression.

7. CRT: A New Kind of Social Justice or Educational Socialism? Examining the philosophy behind CRT, its roots in Marxism, and the impact it has on society by dividing people into oppressors and victims.

8. Does CRT Punish Hard Work? Discussing how CRT discourages individual achievement and the importance of hard work, perseverance, and responsibility in pursuing the American Dream.

9. Hate and Violence: The Dangerous Consequences of Division. Linking CRT to increasing hate and violence, using the Covenant School Shooting as an

example of how divisive ideologies can fuel dangerous actions.

10. Audrey Hale's Manifesto: When Hate Turns Deadly. A closer look at the Covenant School shooter's manifesto and how ideas about race and privilege influenced her actions.

11. Exposing the Agenda: Why CRT is Pushed in Schools. Investigating the motives behind pushing CRT into schools and how global elites use it to divide and conquer society.

12. Critical Legal Studies: Where CRT Began. Tracing the origins of CRT back to the Critical Legal Studies movement and its influence on modern education.

13. Rejecting Meritocracy: Why CRT Opposes Success. How CRT challenges traditional ideas like hard work, meritocracy, and fairness by promoting victimhood and blaming societal structures for inequality.

14. Barack Obama: A Turning Point in Race Relations? Reflecting on the presidency of Barack Obama and how race relations evolved, including ongoing calls for Affirmative Action.

15. Hegemony: The Power of Indoctrination. Exploring Antonio Gramsci's idea of hegemony and how elites use education and culture to spread their ideologies and control society.

16. The Real Goal: Divide and Conquer. Understanding how CRT and similar ideologies are used to create division among people, ultimately serving the interests of global elites.

17. Where It All Began: Prayer and Patriotism. Exploring the idea that the decline of traditional values started when prayer and patriotism were removed from the home, not just schools.

18. The Domino Effect: Losing Faith in the Family. How the erosion of spiritual teachings and American history at home opened the door for harmful ideologies to take root in society.

19. When Courts Took God Out of Schools. A look at the 1962 Supreme Court case *Engel v. Vitale*, which removed prayer from public schools and its lasting impact on education and culture.

20. What Happened After: From Bible Readings to Evolution. How removing prayer led to schools replacing the idea of a Creator with evolutionary theories, creating a sense of purposelessness among students.

21. Learning from History: What Dictators Did. Examining how dictators and communist leaders throughout history have removed religion to weaken societies, drawing parallels to today.

22. Sex Ed Becomes Gender Ed. How introducing sex education in schools opened the door for gender ideology, with explicit content infiltrating classrooms and libraries.

23. Abstinence to Comprehensive: The Shift in Sex Ed. Tracing the shift from teaching abstinence to promoting comprehensive sex education shaped by the feminist movement and Planned Parenthood.

24. SIECUS: How It All Started. The founding of SIECUS in 1964 and how it pushed comprehensive sex education into schools, leading to today's focus on gender ideology.

25. From the Classroom to the Clinic. Examining how current policies under Title IX and the Biden Administration are creating a "school-to-clinic pipeline," where schools facilitate medical decisions without parental consent.

26. Feminism's Role in Rewriting Morality. How the feminist movement, along with Planned Parenthood, replaced traditional moral teachings with ideas that promote sexual freedom and undermine abstinence.

27. A Parent's Role in Teaching Values. Reinforcing the importance of parents, not schools, in teaching children about sex, morality, and spiritual truths.

28. The Dangers of Modern Sex Ed. Addressing the

aggressive and harmful nature of modern sex education and its effects on today's generation.

29. The Bible on Sex: A Spiritual Act. Exploring biblical teachings about the sacredness of sex and why the government shouldn't interfere in teaching this to children.

30. A Call to Action: Reclaiming Our Families. Encouraging families to take back the responsibility of teaching spiritual and moral values to protect children from harmful ideologies.

31. The Decline of Parental Authority. How removing God from society also led to the erosion of parents' rights over their children's upbringing.

32. Thomas Jefferson's Warning. Reflecting on Thomas Jefferson's belief that parents, not the government, should have control over their children's education.

33. Parents Knew Best: Until the 2000s. How parental authority was a cornerstone of American values until recent decades when government influence grew stronger.

34. The Feminist Push: Why Both Parents Left the Home. Exploring how the feminist movement encouraged both parents to work, giving the government more influence over children's minds.

35. "These Are Our Kids": The Government's Claim.

Analyzing how political leaders claim children belong to society, not just their parents, and the implications of that mindset.

36. From Mao to America: Government as "Parent." Drawing parallels between Mao's China and the increasing governmental control over American children.

37. California's "Cradle-to-Career": Government Planning Your Child's Life. Understanding how programs like California's "Cradle-to-Career" aim to shape children's futures from a young age, limiting parental input.

38. Obama's Vision: The Life of Julia. Examining Obama's cradle-to-grave welfare model and its role in replacing family and community with government dependency.

39. The Real Goal: Removing Parental Rights. How government programs and policies aim to diminish parents' control and replace it with state authority.

40. George Washington and the Power of Parenting. Reflecting on George Washington's acknowledgment of his mother's influence and the enduring importance of parental guidance.

41. The Breakdown of the Family: Today's Greatest Problem. Discussing the loss of connection between

parents and children and its consequences for society.

42. Self-Government: Parents Teaching Responsibility. Why parents must instill values of responsibility, hard work, and self-government in their children for a strong future.

43. Teaching Kids to Choose: Life or Death. How the Bible teaches individual responsibility and the importance of parents helping children make wise choices.

44. Taking Responsibility: The Debt Crisis and Abortion. Exploring how society avoids responsibility, from student loans to abortion, and how parental teaching can reverse this trend.

45. Instilling Motivation and Critical Thinking. The role of parents in fostering intrinsic motivation and independent thinking in their children to help them succeed.

46. Conversations That Matter: Why TV Isn't Enough. The importance of dinner table discussions on Biblical values and worldview as a tool for strengthening family bonds and wisdom.

47. The Parent's Role in Civic Engagement. Why involving parents in civic matters is key to engaging the next generation and shaping a better future.

48. A Wake-Up Call at College Orientation. Penny Nance's experience at a freshman orientation reveals the dominance of pronoun politics at universities today.

49. The Problem with Pronouns: Identity Politics on Campus. How forcing students and teachers to use preferred pronouns is affecting free speech and religious beliefs at public universities.

50. From Harvard's Holy Beginnings to a Radical Shift. Tracing Harvard's transformation from a school founded on biblical principles to a hub of anti-Christian and anti-white sentiment.

51. Harvard's Mission: From God to "Abolish the White Race." Exploring Harvard's radical shift from its religious foundations to publishing controversial articles in the 21st century.

52. Higher Education's Original Purpose. Looking back at how universities once prioritized teaching the Bible, truth, and moral guidance before the secular shift.

53. Public Education's New Agenda. How public education today focuses on teaching students what to think, not how to think, and the consequences of this indoctrination.

54. The Real Goal of Public Education? Questioning the true purpose of public education based on H.L.

Mencken's view that it aims to standardize citizens and suppress originality.

55. Parents, Protect Your Kids: Stop Sending Them to the Lion's Den. Urging parents to reconsider sending their children to state-sponsored schools where they risk being indoctrinated rather than educated.

56. Don't Believe the Lie: Can Kids Be a Light in Public Schools? Debunking the idea that sending children to public school will make them a "light in the darkness" when, more often, they are the ones being influenced.

57. Taking Action: Eliminating the Department of Education. A call to action to abolish the Department of Education, claiming it's beyond fixing and no longer serves students or parents.

CHAPTER SEVEN:
ABORTION

1. The Beginning of the Debate: Overpopulation and Birth Control. How Thomas Malthus' ideas of population control led to the rise of birth control and the fear of overpopulation.

2. Eugenics: The Dark Side of Population Control. Exploring how the Eugenics Movement sought to eliminate "unfit" members of society, separating people by their perceived worth.

3. Margaret Sanger: The Founder of Planned Parenthood. How Margaret Sanger's push for birth control and eugenics led to the founding of Planned Parenthood and shaped modern views on abortion.

4. Sanger's Mission: Birth Control as a Tool for Racial Control. Revealing Margaret Sanger's racist roots and how she used birth control as a way to promote eugenics and population control.

5. From Birth Control to Planned Parenthood. The creation of Planned Parenthood and its global impact on family planning, birth control, and abortion.

6. The Rockefellers and the Global Push for Population Control. How wealthy elites like the Rockefellers funded Sanger's efforts to spread birth control and abortion worldwide.

7. The Harmful Effects of Birth Control on Young Women. Examining the physical and mental health risks of birth control pills, particularly for teenage girls.

8. Planned Parenthood's Recent Shift: Denouncing Sanger's Legacy. How Planned Parenthood now distances itself from Margaret Sanger's eugenicist beliefs while continuing to promote reproductive rights.

9. The Ever-Changing Narrative: Climate Change and Reproductive Rights. How political language and nar-

ratives around climate change and reproductive health evolve to create confusion while maintaining the same goals.

10. Betty Friedan and the Feminist Push for Abortion. How radical feminist Betty Friedan connected the women's rights movement to the push for legalizing abortion in the 1960s.

11. Feminism and Abortion Rights: NOW and NARAL. The role of feminist organizations like NOW and NARAL in advocating for reproductive rights and the legalization of abortion.

12. *Roe v. Wade:* The Turning Point. How the landmark Supreme Court case *Roe v. Wade* in 1973 affirmed women's rights to abortion and shaped national laws.

13. *Griswold v. Connecticut:* The Start of Legal Birth Control. How the 1965 Supreme Court case allowed married couples access to contraception and set the stage for more reproductive rights cases.

14. Title X: Government-Funded Family Planning Begins. The introduction of Title X in 1970, which funded family planning and sex education programs across the United States.

15. Eisenstadt v. Baird: Contraceptives for Everyone. The 1972 Supreme Court ruling that allowed contracep-

tives to be available to all, regardless of marital status.

16. *Roe v. Wade:* The Case That Changed Everything. The landmark 1973 Supreme Court decision that legalized abortion in all fifty states and reshaped American society.

17. The Rise of the Abortion Industry. How abortion became a multi-billion dollar industry with the approval of the abortion pill, hormone therapy, and over-the-counter Plan B.

18. The Gag Rule: Bush vs. Planned Parenthood. President George W. Bush's reinstatement of the gag rule, restricting government funding for abortions, and the backlash from pro-choice advocates.

19. The Return of Reproductive Health: Obama's Overturn. President Barack Obama's reversal of the gag rule, signaling his administration's commitment to protecting reproductive rights.

20. First Trimester Abortions: The Abortion Pill. A detailed look at the abortion pill, how it works, and why it's considered controversial.

21. Second Trimester Abortions: Dilation and Evacuation. Breaking down the D&E abortion procedure, from how it's performed to the risks involved for the

mother.

22. Third Trimester Abortions: Induction and D&E. Exploring the most extreme and risky forms of abortion in the third trimester, including the method of injecting lethal substances into the baby.

23. The Gruesome Reality: Why Abortion Videos Are Hidden. Why the truth about abortion procedures is often hidden from the public, and how exposing the reality changes perspectives.

24. The Impact of Abortion on Women. The physical and psychological toll of abortion on women, supported by research and studies showing long-term mental health effects.

25. Abortion's Toll on Men and Fathers. Exploring how abortion affects men, with insights into the emotional and psychological struggles faced by fathers post-abortion.

26. A Psychiatrist's Perspective: The Hidden Trauma. The testimony of a psychiatrist who performed abortions and witnessed the lasting trauma it caused in women, even if they thought it was the "right choice."

27. The Spiritual War: Abortion as Defiance Against God. Addressing the spiritual side of the abortion de-

bate, how it's seen as defiance against the Creator, and why it fuels such deep divisions.

28. First Trimester: The Beginning of Life. How the fertilized egg grows into an embryo, forming the amniotic sac, placenta, and early organs within the first twelve weeks.

29. Little Miracles: Heartbeats and Tiny Limbs. Highlighting the formation of facial features, the development of sensory organs, and the baby's heartbeat by week six.

30. Second Trimester: Baby Takes Shape. How the baby's fingers, toes, and facial features become distinct, and the ability to identify the baby's gender develops around week twenty.

31. The Vernix Caseosa: God's Amazing Protection. The wonder of the whitish coating that protects the baby's skin from the amniotic fluid and how it shows the beauty of God's design.

32. Third Trimester: Getting Ready for the World. The final weeks of pregnancy when the baby's brain rapidly grows, lungs develop, and the baby gains full reflexes and senses.

33. A Baby's Life Begins at Conception. Presenting the scientific testimony from experts who confirm that

human life begins at conception, supported by biblical references.

34. Abortion: A Modern-Day Slavery. Drawing a parallel between abortion and slavery as two dehumanizing practices that devalue human life and defy God's design.

35. The Reality of "Medical" Abortions. Uncovering the truth about so-called "medical" abortions, where the term is misused to describe the intentional killing of a baby.

36. *The Silent Scream:* The Truth About Abortion. Dr. Bernard Nathanson's powerful testimony and his film *The Silent Scream*, showing the horrifying reality of abortion.

37. Abortion and Constitutional Rights. Addressing how abortion violates the baby's constitutional right to life, contradicting the values enshrined in the U.S. Constitution.

38. Bodily Autonomy vs. A Baby's Right to Life. Debunking the argument that abortion is about "bodily autonomy" by presenting the science of DNA and the uniqueness of the unborn child.

39. Pregnancy Centers vs. Planned Parenthood. Comparing pregnancy centers that offer real support to women with Planned Parenthood's focus on abortion

and lack of post-abortion care.

40. The Feminist Movement's Lie. Exposing the false idea promoted by the feminist movement that women need abortion to succeed, and how this devalues both life and motherhood.

41. The Emotional Toll of Abortion. Exploring the psychological impact of abortion on women and men, revealing long-term effects like depression, anxiety, and regret.

42. A Nation Under Judgment. Reflecting on how abortion is a modern-day version of child sacrifice and the spiritual consequences for a nation that devalues life.

CHAPTER 8:
THE GREATEST ISSUE
FACING AMERICA

1. A World Deceived: The Cost of Rejecting Truth. The challenge of standing up for biblical principles in a world where truth is distorted and rejected.

2. The Destruction of the Family: Satan's Master Plan. How Satan is undermining God's design for the family by distorting male and female roles and promoting broken homes.

3. Why the Family Is the Foundation of Society. Exploring the biblical definition of the nuclear family and how its breakdown leads to societal collapse.

4. The Devil's Strategy: Breaking Down the Nuclear Family. A look at how Satan's tactics mirror the deception in the Garden of Eden and target the foundation of strong families.

5. Roles Reversed: When Men Stop Leading and Women Abandon the Home. How abandoning traditional gender roles has contributed to the collapse of the family and societal confusion.

6. God's First Institution: The Family. The importance of the family as the first institution created by God and the biblical command to be fruitful and multiply.

7. Redefining Family: The Dangerous Philosophy of Relativism. How the world's fluid definition of family and marriage creates confusion and undermines biblical truth.

8. The Overpopulation Myth: The Truth About Climate and Population Control. Debunking the fearmongering narrative about overpopulation and how global elites push population control as a solution.

9. Normalizing Sin: How Society Has Legalized Immorality. How the legalization of abortion, same-sex marriage, and other sins has seared the nation's con-

science and led to moral decay.

10. Communism and the Family: The Ultimate Target. Exploring how communist ideologies aim to dismantle the family to control society, and why strong families are the greatest threat to tyrants.

11. Marriage as God Intended: The Covenant of One Man and One Woman. How marriage, as a covenant created by God, is essential for building a strong nation and why any other definition leads to chaos.

12. The Decline of Two-Parent Households. Reviewing the statistics on the decline of children growing up with both parents and the consequences for future generations.

13. Children Without Fathers: The Cost of Broken Families. How the absence of fathers in the home leads to higher rates of crime, drug abuse, and suicide among children.

14. Easy Divorce: The Path to Family Breakdown. The impact of no-fault divorce laws on marriage stability and how they have contributed to the family crisis in America.

15. Communism's War on Marriage and Religion. Understanding how Karl Marx and other communists targeted marriage and religion to dismantle societal

structures and gain control.

16. The Gender Equality Myth: Communism's Destructive Agenda. How gender equality, as promoted by communism and radical feminism, is being used to blur gender distinctions and weaken families.

17. The Need for Strong Families: A Path to National Restoration. Why the future of America depends on restoring the traditional family and how that is the key to preserving freedom and moral order.

18. Feminism's True Impact: More Than Equal Rights? A closer look at the real consequences of the feminist movement beyond the popular narrative of equal pay and voting rights.

19. The 1960s Revolution: When Roles Began to Change. How the feminist movement and sexual liberation in the 1960s reshaped the traditional roles of men and women in society.

20. The Myth of Free Love: What Really Happened. The dark side of the "free love" movement and how it led to the breakdown of sexual morality and family stability.

21. Betty Friedan's Flame: The Feminine Mystique and Its Legacy. Examining Betty Friedan's influence on feminism, her critique of the family, and how her radi-

cal ideas reshaped womanhood.

22. The Communist Connection: Feminism's Roots in Marxism. How feminist leaders had ties to socialist and communist ideologies and what that means for the movement's real goals.

23. Liberation or Lies? The Feminist Promise. Unpacking the feminist claim of "liberation" and whether it has truly delivered on its promises to women.

24. Women in the Workforce: Did the Feminist Dream Deliver? How the feminist push for women in the workforce changed the dynamic of the family and its lasting effects on women's happiness.

25. More Than Taxes: Why Feminists Wanted Women in the Workforce. The hidden agenda behind getting women out of the home and into the workplace, beyond just increased tax revenue.

26. The Children Pay: What Happens When Mothers Leave the Home. How the feminist movement's push for careers over family impacted the next generation of children.

27. Communism and Feminism: Partners in Breaking Down the Family. How communism and feminism work together to dismantle the traditional family structure and blur gender roles.

28. "You Don't Need a Man!": Feminism's Biggest Lie. How feminism's rejection of men and traditional roles has led to unhappiness and confusion for women.

29. The Feminist Trap: Is "Personal Satisfaction" a Scam? Questioning whether the feminist movement's call for women to prioritize careers and independence has truly led to happiness.

30. The Real Cost of Feminism: Broken Families and Unhappy Women. Statistics and studies showing the emotional and societal toll of the feminist movement on women and families.

31. Radical Feminism Today: What NOW Really Stands For. The modern feminist movement's focus on abortion, LGBTQ rights, and redefining womanhood, and why it might be the most anti-woman group in America.

32. The War on Masculinity: How Feminism Changed the Game. A look at how feminism has reshaped society's view of men and masculinity, leading to a crisis in male identity.

33. Media and the Weak Man: Dads in Sitcoms and Beyond. How TV shows and movies portray fathers as bumbling fools, and the damaging effects this has on male confidence and leadership.

34. Independent Women and Passive Men: A Role Reversal. The feminist message of "women don't need men" and how it has caused men to retreat from their God-given roles as leaders.

35. Toxic or Strong? The Real Meaning of Masculinity. Debunking the myth of "toxic masculinity" and explaining why strong, godly men are needed more than ever in today's world.

36. Why Weak Men Are Dangerous: Masculinity in Crisis. The dangers of men becoming passive, docile, and emotionally driven in a world that needs protectors and leaders.

37. Adam's Failure: Learning from the First Man's Mistake. What Adam's failure to protect Eve in the Garden teaches us about the need for men to guard their families and lead with strength.

38. Dylan Mulvaney and the Feminization of Men. Exploring the cultural trend of men embracing femininity and why it's leaving women unsatisfied and society unbalanced.

39. Alpha vs. Beta: What It Really Means to Be a Man. Understanding the true difference between alpha males and beta boys, and why real leadership has nothing to do with muscles.

40. The Hero Archetype: What Women Really Want. How women instinctively seek strong, courageous men who protect and provide, and why this ideal still resonates today.

41. Raising Boys in a Confused World: Where Are the Role Models? The challenges boys face growing up without strong male role models to teach them how to embrace manhood.

42. Why Society Needs Masculinity: The Role of the Protector. The vital role of men as protectors, leaders, and providers in both the family and society and why masculinity is essential to a healthy culture.

43. Feminism and the Breakdown of Gender Roles. How the feminist movement blurred the lines between male and female roles, leading to confusion and instability in society.

44. Women's Role in the Gender Confusion Crisis. A candid look at how women's demands for equality in everything contributed to the erosion of clear gender roles, and what can be done to restore balance.

45. The Globalist Agenda: How Weak Men Serve the Elites. Why the push for weak, feminized men benefits global elites by making society easier to control, and how men can fight back.

46. Boxing Blowout: How Gender Ideology Hurt Women's Sports. The story of Angela Carini and the effects of allowing men in women's sports.

47. Feminism's Role in the Gender Debate. How the feminist movement helped pave the way for LGBTQ activism and gender ideology.

48. The Rainbow Cult: A New Religious Movement. How LGBTQ activism has become a powerful, almost religious, force in society, and what happens to those who don't conform.

49. Weaponizing Mental Health: The LGBTQ Agenda. How the movement manipulates mental health struggles to push a broader agenda, ignoring the real issues people face.

50. The Destruction of the Family: Gay Marriage and Its Impact. Why legalizing gay marriage hurt the nuclear family and opened the door to more societal issues.

51. A Marxist Plot: The LGBTQ Agenda's Communist Roots. Tracing LGBTQ activism back to communist leaders and their plans to destroy the family unit.

52. Strong Families, Strong Economy. How strong family units contribute to a thriving economy and why the breakdown of the family weakens society.

53. Why Marriage Matters: The Economic Benefits of Two-Parent Homes. The data behind why married families are financially better off and how it helps children succeed.

54. Motivating Men: How Marriage Drives Success. Studies show married men work harder and earn more—why this matters for society.

55. Single Parenthood: The Hidden Cost to Children and Society. How the rise of single-parent homes has led to increased poverty and fewer opportunities for children.

56. Communism's Influence on Family Breakdown. How secular individualism and communist ideas have infiltrated our institutions, leading to the collapse of traditional family values.

57. Government Encouragement: Why Staying Single Pays More. How government welfare programs incentivize single motherhood and undermine family stability.

58. Restoring the American Dream: How Strong Families Create Prosperity. The link between two-parent households and economic success, and why rebuilding the family is key to restoring the American Dream.

59. A Question I Keep Getting Asked. What sparked my passion for the truth?"

60. It All Starts at Home. The power of family discussions and togetherness.

61. The Real Problem: Disconnected Families: Why are we glued to our phones and not to each other?

62. Losing Our Way: The College Trap. Why so many young people lose their moral compass.

63. Educating Your Kids: The World vs. The Word of God. You choose what will shape your life.

64. Winning Your Kids' Hearts Back. Putting away distractions from your children and teaching them why.

65. Making Family Time Count. How to make learning fun and children engaged.

66. Fighting the Left's Attack on Strong Families. Why the world tries to undermine your children's values.

67. Is It Okay to Believe What Your Parents Believe? Standing by your parents doesn't mean you're brainwashed.

68. Choosing Truth Over Culture's Lies. Why following biblical wisdom is preferable to the culture's confusion.

CHAPTER 9:
HOW IN THE WORLD DID WE GET HERE?

1. Is This Real Life? About these unprecedented times and changes.

2. How Did We Get Here? What happens when a nation forgets its roots.

3. The Bigger Plan: It's Not a Conspiracy, It's an Agenda. Understanding the push towards global control.

4. Freedom Comes From God, Not Government. Why our liberties depend on recognizing God's authority.

5. When Strong Men Fall, Weakness Takes Over. The cycle of strong vs. weak men throughout history.

6. Religion and Politics: They Were Never Separate. Why keeping religion out of politics is hurting us.

7. Has the Church Lost Its Voice? How the Church's silence is leading us astray.

8. When Truth Gets Twisted. How culture's redefinition of truth is leading to chaos.

9. Strong Families, Strong Nation. Why the breakdown of the family is the real crisis.

10. Apathy and Complacency: Our Biggest Enemies. Why we can't ignore the fight for our values.

11. Why I Choose to Stand. Speaking up for truth and defending freedom.

12. Freedom: A Responsibility, Not a Right. What our forefathers fought for.

13. What William Bradford Can Teach Gen Z. About the courage to choose the right path.

14. Stop Complaining, Start Acting. How to turn dreams into reality.

15. We've Been Lied To. Exposing the myths GenZ has been fed.

16. Why Asking Questions Is Powerful. About challenging everything and staying curious.

17. Find Your Passion and Get Involved. Be the change in your community.

18. Dress Like You Care. How to make an impact with your presence.

19. Learn Your History, Defend Your Future. Why knowing the past matters.

20. Take a Worldview Check. Making sure you're thinking biblically.

21. Christians Have to Vote. Our responsibility is to uphold righteousness.

22. Be Bold for Christ. How to stand like David in a world of giants.

23. Never Stand Alone. The power of courage and conviction.

24. Saving Our Republic: Your Personal Role. How are you preserving your freedom?

25. We Are the Last Defense. It's up to "We the People."

To Contact

Hannah Faulkner

www.cultureof1776.com
www.rumble.com/c/TheHannahFaulknerShow
www.hannahfaulkner1776.substack.com